Exploring God's Promises

HOPE

Inspiring True Stories
of
God's Promise Fulfilled

EDITORS OF GUIDEPOSTS

Guideposts

Exploring God's Promises: Hope

Published by Guideposts Books
100 Reserve Road, Suite E200
Danbury, CT 06810
Guideposts.org

Acknowledgments

Every attempt has been made to credit the sources of copyrighted material used in this book. If any such acknowledgment has been inadvertently omitted or miscredited, receipt of such information would be appreciated.

Cover design by Serena Fox, Bean Inc.
Interior design by Serena Fox, Bean Inc.
Cover illustration © Irina Grabovaya, Shutterstock
Typeset by Aptara, Inc.

ISBN 978-1-961125-81-0 (hardcover)
ISBN 978-1-965859-78-0 (softcover)
ISBN 978-1-961125-82-7 (epub)

Printed and bound in the United States of America

Gather the riches of God's promises.
Nobody can take away from you those texts
from the Bible which you have learned by heart.

—Corrie ten Boom

CONTENTS

Preface 6
A Higher Hope
By Heidi Gaul

When Flamingos Take Flight 14
By Lynne Hartke

After the Storm 20
By Jennie Ivey

It Can All Change in a Day 25
By Michelle Stiffler

The Desire of My Heart 31
By Maureen Miller

Flourish Like a Palm Tree 40
By Mindy Baker

Back to This Place 45
By Cathy Bryant

Remember How Far You've Come 52
By Laurie Davies

The Eagles Are Coming 60
By Sarah Greek

Light in the Dark Sky 65
By Darlene Kerr

Protection for the Passage 70
By Eryn Lynum

Hands of the Father 78
By Samuel Pennock

The Day I Found Hope 83
By Amy Catlin Wozniak

God's Formula for Hope 89
By Denise Margaret Ackerman

Finding Forgiveness, One Word at a Time 95
By Rebecca Hastings

A Work in Progress 102
By Jennifer Hutmire

A Heart Full of God. 107
By Kathie Kania

The Anniversary Trip 112
By Amanda Pennock

Our Divine Travel Guide. 117
By Claire McGarry

Provision Awaits on the Other Side 123
By Kenneth Avon White

Beautiful in Its Time 129
By Adria Wilkins

A Vision for Moving Forward 136
By Eryn Lynum

Faith, Hope, and Love 142
By Heather Jepsen

Joy in the Morning 150
By Elsa Kok Colopy

Hope-Filled Prayers. 155
By Bettie Boswell

Saying Thank You to Life 160
By Roberta Messner

An Unexpected Path to Personal Healing 168
By Cristina Moore

Finding Hope in the Waiting 174
By Amanda Hayhurst

He Has a Good Plan 179
By Emily Carol Marszalek

Smiley Face Mail 185
By Elsa Kok Colopy

Baby Steps of Hope 192
By April Strauch

Expanding My Net 198
By Claire McGarry

Turned Around in the Desert 204
By Lynne Hartke

Music to God's Ears 212
By Linda S. Clare

Healing Promises 218
By Amy Wallace

Hope in the Midst of Chaos 223
By Heather Jepsen

From Tongue-Tied to Tenacious 230
By Bettie Boswell

Strong and Courageous 236
By Chris Maday Schmidt

Biblical Promises of Hope 242

PREFACE

A HIGHER HOPE

By Heidi Gaul

WHY IS HOPE important? What makes it a such a valuable component to our well-being?

Merriam-Webster's dictionary defines hope as: "to desire with expectation of obtainment or fulfillment" and "to cherish a desire with anticipation; to want something to happen or be true." That sounds a lot like simple optimism. Psychologists say that hope is not actually an emotion—that it is a way of thinking. We often say we "feel" hopeful, yet hope is not just wishing for positive outcomes, nor is it ignoring problems as if they'll go away on their own. Hope involves the ability to find alternative ways to reach goals, despite facing significant challenges. It's persevering to make things happen and the belief that success can be reached.

Hope is formidable. Trusting in and planning on positive results aids our mental health, with one added by-product being improved physical fitness. When we believe things will go well, they do—on every level. This simple change of attitude packs a punch!

When hope is combined with faith, the result becomes immeasurably greater. How often do we read a headline featuring an uplifting occurrence we'd deemed impossible, or listen as a pastor mentions a miracle made real? With God guiding our choices, "all things are possible" (Matthew 19:26, NIV).

Hope is a lifeline for faith, one God created to pull believers through tough times. "Not only so, but we also glory in our sufferings, because we know that suffering produces perseverance; perseverance, character; and character, hope" (Romans 5:3–4, NIV). How insightful for Paul, in his Letter to the Romans, to have named hope as the ultimate positive emotion for Christians to experience. Is there anything more freeing, more enduring?

A Promise of Hope

God. Promises. Hope. Whether we take these words one by one or all together, without them our lives would be empty. Separately, they represent who we are in Christ. Together, they create the sacred intersection where power and grace meet faith. God promises hope. It really is that simple.

What compels God to gift us with promises? And why does He offer us so many of them—more than 7,000? Because He knows us. He is aware of the challenges we face and our fear of abandonment. He understands we need the unshakable hope only He can provide. Our resolve can waver under the weight of frustration, fear, pain, and grief. Even mundane, everyday disappointments sap our enthusiasm. D. L. Moody put it well: "God never made a promise that was too good to be true."

How can we maintain a sense of hope during times of trial? We can do it by keeping our focus on God, by putting our faith in His promises. He is the sole source of true hope, and we can find it between the Bible's covers, revealed in stories of real people with real problems. The challenges they battled are similar to those we face today, whether emotional, physical, spiritual, or material. Likewise, the choices they made and the solutions they found provide reassurance of God's unfailing devotion.

The day my doctor's office notified me of a fast-growing cancerous tumor in my breast, Jesus set about transforming me, inside and out. At first, my emotions read like a winter weather report: stormy, wet, and unpredictable. But as the days of treatment and surgery moved toward weeks and months, a steadfast determination and acceptance of His will replaced my terror. I understood His plans for me were good and eternal (Jeremiah 29:11). The results of that challenge—an abiding faith and unflappable hope—signaled a permanent change in my point of view, one I've come to accept with humility and deep gratitude.

Often, during that difficult period, I reflected on the woman who reached for Jesus's cloak as He walked along a crowded street (Matthew 9:20–22). Due to her constant bleeding, this woman was considered unclean. Her suffering had continued for years, whereas my situation transpired over months. Yet I related to her. People avoided contact with her. My cancer diagnosis made some people uncomfortable and as a result, my circle of friends shrank. This woman and I shared the seeming senselessness of the situation, but we also shared the priceless hope we placed in Jesus. She didn't hesitate to reach out for His help. Nor did I. His healing touch encompassed more than my diseased breast—it addressed my fears and sorrows, my brokenness.

My life has taken on a greater purpose than I ever conceived possible. I won't know until I meet her in heaven, but I suspect He did the same for that unnamed woman of faith. He can do the same for all of us as we reach out to Him in hope.

Still, there are times when the world we inhabit can seem crazy, as if it were spinning out of control. How can things get so off-kilter? Wars, grief, illness, poverty—the agonizing list can appear long. At times, life's problems prove overwhelming, and leave us with little hope for the future. But when we search for something solid to hold onto, we find a rock to keep us steady in the shifting sands. We can live in joy and security through Jesus and the hope He provides. As Martin Luther King Jr. said, "We must accept finite disappointment, but never lose infinite hope."

After my husband suffered a serious fall resulting in a traumatic brain injury, my quiet, simple world didn't just spin crazily out of orbit. It flipped upside down. Doctor visits, physical and occupational therapy, juggling multiple medications, and exhaustion filled our time. The circumstances we found ourselves in were not what we'd planned—far from it. And yet, it was as if God took each of us by the hand and walked us through the situation and past the pain, tears, and fears. He carried us beyond our loss to a slower lifestyle He'd chosen just for us, one where we'd be better suited to honor Him. We clung to the words of hope found in Psalm 23:4 (NIV): "Even though I walk through the darkest valley, I will fear no evil, for you are with me; your rod and your staff, they comfort me." In God, we found hope, our faith resting securely in His promises.

Hope Grounded in the Bible

God reaches out to reassure us through the words of the Bible. The sacred books contained between its covers offer answers to any hardship we might encounter. Countless men and women coped with negative experiences as varied—and as relevant—as those we battle in our current times. We can learn from their authentic responses, both righteous and flawed.

We see fear and hatred overcome by courage, perseverance, and faith. Like a fountain of wisdom, we can drink in these godly traits and apply them to our own circumstances. Let's explore a couple of these characters.

It's easy to think of Bible characters like Joseph (Genesis 30:24–50:26). If ever a story of perpetual hope in the midst of adversity existed, it can be found in the chapters about this brave, humble man. He bore the jealousy and almost murderous betrayal of his brothers, just for being his father's favorite. How many of us have lingered on the wrong end of that seesaw longer than necessary? Whether concerning family, friends, or career, I've sometimes found myself eyeing other's "coats of many colors." Then, when a rainbow jacket of my own becomes available, I discover the fit is off or that it is something I no longer desire.

Yet Joseph had hope. I wonder if he knew just what he hoped for, or if he simply hoped. He had so little, and yet after being rescued from the pit he'd been abandoned to, life seemed as if it might improve. Then while Joseph was serving in slavery, Potiphar's wife falsely accused him of rape. He was found guilty. Still, he trusted in God's promises and held on. During Joseph's resultant time spent in prison, his God-given ability to interpret dreams was made known to the Pharaoh. When Joseph's advice to put food aside for an upcoming famine was heeded, he was appointed to the highest position under the crown. Joseph married, had children, and reunited with his estranged family. His decades of trial finished in a testimony of love, forgiveness, and hope for the ages.

G. K. Chesterton said, "To love means loving the unlovable. To forgive means pardoning the unpardonable. Faith means believing in the unbelievable. Hope means hoping when everything seems hopeless." These words describe Joseph's life well.

Mary, mother of Jesus, also comes to mind. This sweet girl, probably in her early teens, was engaged to be married to Joseph, a carpenter and a man of honor. At that point, her future seemed to be set out for her, until her life turned upside down. When the angel Gabriel spoke of God's plan for her to give birth to the Messiah, she surrendered to His will. Mary believed in the promises she heard. She knew she would face trials, both in regard to her unwed pregnancy and the magnitude of being our Savior's mother. Despite all the struggles in her life, she held on to the eternal hope she found in her son, Jesus. A hope born of God. What can we glean from her willingness to obey and trust? Is it possible that hope comes not just from perseverance but also from forgiveness like Joseph's or obedience like Mary's?

Joseph and Mary are two of the Bible's key characters. But sometimes we see hope come in smaller, less recognizable packages. We read about Moses's mother, Jochebed. When Pharaoh commanded all infant sons to be cast into the river, she placed her baby in a basket and hid it in the reeds. What dared she hope for? His chances for survival seemed slim, yet God rescued her son through the love of the Pharaoh's own daughter. He even made it possible for Jochebed to wet-nurse baby Moses (Exodus 1:22–2:10).

Hope for Today

Hope isn't always bound together with visions and miracles, nor is it exclusive to ancient times. But I do believe that like any aspect of God's love, it is often best revealed in stories. These Bible stories show the poignancy of being on both the receiving and the giving end as we embody the hands of God. And there are times when His touch of hope is profoundly sublime.

The collection you are about to read is made up of the writings of people you might meet at the grocery store, church, or work. The lives they lead are similar to many of ours. These people saw God's touch in their circumstances and believed in a successful outcome for their situations, whether a tale of holding onto faith despite health or financial challenges or of clinging to God's promises through loneliness or confusion. This group of believers saw a spark of hope in the midst of their lives and generously shared it. I'm so glad they did.

I trust you'll see yourself and your circumstances mirrored in one or more of these stories. You'll be heartened as you read of God's deliverance from various problems and strengthened in the knowledge that we can depend on Him. He still performs miracles—we only need to watch for them. Norman Vincent Peale put it this way: "Become a possibilitarian. No matter how dark things seem to be or actually are, raise your sights and see possibilities—always see them, for they're always there." God keeps His promises. Every. Single. One.

Hope is raining down on all of us like confetti at a parade. It's forming drifts in the corners of our lives and building up underfoot. It's time to tuck away our umbrellas, lift our faces heavenward, stretch our arms wide, and turn our palms up to grasp for every bit of it. Let's celebrate as it gets caught in our hair, our circumstances, and our hearts.

The LORD will guide you always; he will satisfy your needs in a sun-scorched land and will strengthen your frame. You will be like a well-watered garden, like a spring whose waters never fail.

Isaiah 58:11 (NIV)

WHEN FLAMINGOS TAKE FLIGHT

By Lynne Hartke

"ARE WE SURE THIS IS the right way?" I asked my son, Nate, who was driving his wife, Rachel, their two young children, Madelyn and Micah, and me across an endless wasteland in the middle of the Atacama Desert in northern Chile. We had left the two-lane paved road several miles back and had not seen another car since we turned onto a dusty dirt road—unless we counted the discarded shells of rusted-out vehicles in what seemed a post-apocalyptic landscape. We prayed the coordinates we had downloaded that morning would get us to our destination.

I peered to the left. Desert.

I gazed to the right. Desert.

No matter which way I turned, there was no sign of life of any vegetation on the horizon. As the miles increased, so did the nervousness in the car.

"How much farther?"

"Shouldn't we be there already?"

"What if we run out of gas?"

Nate checked the gas gauge as he white-knuckled the steering wheel, trying to avoid the worst bumps on the potholed dirt road. "I have my wife, two toddlers, and my mother in this car," he mumbled, "and we are wandering around in the middle of a desert."

And not just any desert, but one of the driest locations on Earth.

"When was the last time it rained?" we had asked the locals when we arrived at San Pedro the night before.

"It rained for three minutes last summer."

We had shaken our heads in disbelief at the description of an area that receives less than a tenth of an inch of rain a year, making the Sonoran Desert in our home state of Arizona seem like an oasis of abundance in comparison.

"Take the next right," Rachel instructed as we turned onto one more dirt road.

"I see cars ahead," Nate said with relief. Several minutes later, he parked our rental car next to two tour buses. With our hands full of hats, water bottles, and sunscreen, we stepped out of our air-conditioned sanctuary at our destination—Los Flamencos National Reserve.

The morning sun sharpened to a hard glare. Salt flats dotted the endless brown of the desert, like an unquenchable dehydrator sucking up moisture.

I swallowed. Hard. Why had we come to this godforsaken place?

• • •

Godforsaken? As a pastor's wife for more than three decades, the phrase was not one I threw around lightly. Verses I had learned in years of Sunday school and Bible study had taught me how the entire Earth is filled with God's glory and that God has created His world to be good.

But goodness and glory had not been my experience in the past year, with the death of my dad followed nine months later by the death of my mom. I kicked at the dusty path as dirt sifted into my shoes. The dryness matched my own parched faith. I had maintained the disciplines of reading my Bible, attending church, and prayer, but I had struggled to find a sip of relief from the intense grief. I had welcomed the trip to Chile to visit my son and family while Nate was on a work assignment, seeking a resurgence of hope. Of joy. Of life.

My faith was as arid as the ground beneath my feet.

• • •

"Where's the water?" Micah asked, looking for the promised lake from the website.

"Maybe it's up ahead," his dad said, leading the way down a narrow path.

I bit my tongue before making a snarky comment. Besides the water bottles in our hands, the only water that existed in this inhospitable environment was in our cooler back in the car. Sweat beaded on my top lip but evaporated before I could lick it away. What possible reason would tourists come to this endless expanse of salted nothingness? Why had we?

I realized I should have asked more questions when Rachel set our itinerary. Why weren't we visiting the granite pillars and azure lakes of Torres del Paine? Or the rolling hillsides and vineyards in the Elqui Valley? Or the historical cathedrals and museums in Santiago, the capital city?

Micah ran ahead, his three-year-old legs racing out the wiggles of too many hours in the car. His eighteen-month-old sister, Madelyn, toddled behind.

"Water!" Micah exclaimed.

He was right. Against a stark landscape, the Chaxa Lagoon loomed in front of us—the shallow lake framed by distant, snowcapped mountains. Voices in German, Italian, and Spanish mingled with our English as we joined people from around the world, their binoculars focused on the unmistakable pink flamingos feeding in the saline lagoons.

Heat waves shimmered on the salt flats, distorting the outlines of the three types of flamingos found at the reserve—the brilliant pink Chilean flamingo, the smaller James, and the yellow-legged Andean. With our cell phones as our only cameras, we stood apart from the multicultural bird-watchers who had come to capture photographs of the pink-hued waterfowl. Unperturbed, the birds feasted on microorganisms and brine shrimp in the water, the food responsible for the birds' famous color.

"Drink, please," Micah said—a reasonable request in one of the driest places in the world, but he did not ask in a bird-watching reverent voice, but with toddler urgency. Photographers with impressive lenses on expensive cameras turned and scowled, their collective gaze hotter than the noonday sun.

"Shh," Rachel murmured, hoping to avoid a toddler breakdown as she handed a water bottle to him and his sister.

"Can you stand on one leg like a flamingo?" I whispered after they quenched their thirst.

Biting his lip in concentration, Micah attempted, while Madelyn copied. One leg up. Then the other.

I smiled, because while a group of flamingos is called a stand, my grandchildren were not doing a good job as they tried to balance in the unfamiliar position. They weaved. They tottered. They wobbled.

Like my faith, I thought.

• • •

Like my faith.

The truth settled into a deep place inside me. I might have experienced only one leg on the ground since the death of my parents, but I was still standing. Maybe not as strong as I wished, but God had not abandoned me in the aridness of my dehydrated soul.

Hope stirred. The first I had experienced in months. Maybe only a tiny gulp of hope, but it was hope, nonetheless.

"Let's try one more time," I said to Micah and Madelyn. This time, I joined them, one leg up and wobbly, but still standing.

Still standing.

Having had enough of calisthenics, Micah and Madelyn ran down the path toward the lake before any of us could grab them. Their toddler eyes saw so much that I had missed in my salt-encrusted poverty.

Water!

White soil!

Birds!

In the eyes of a child, Los Flamencos was not a barren wasteland, but a place of beauty despite harsh conditions. Micah's shouting exuberance set to flight a flock of birds. With their long necks extended, the pink flamingos appeared to run across the surface of the lake, water droplets spraying, until their wings sent them airborne.

Cameras clicked around us, capturing an instant in time, of the birds, the salt flats, and distant mountains. My eyes returned to the shallow saline lake to a lone Chilean flamingo who had learned to thrive in a sparse environment. The bird stood, balancing on one leg in the water.

As sure as my own one-legged faith.

Prayer for a Hope-Filled Life

Dear Jesus, give flight to hope today as I practice standing on my one-legged faith, with eyes wide open to beauty, despite my hard places. Amen.

Be strong and courageous. . . for the Lord your God goes with you; he will never leave you nor forsake you.

Deuteronomy 31:6 (NIV)

AFTER THE STORM

By Jennie Ivey

IT WAS THE MIDDLE of the night when my cell phone sounded an ear-piercing alarm. Groggy and confused, I switched on the bedside lamp, picked up the phone, and read these words: "Tornado warning for middle Tennessee. Seek safe shelter immediately." Powerful twisters had touched down in Nashville and were heading straight for the county where I live. I whistled for my dog and together we hurried downstairs to the basement, with three words repeating themselves over and over in my head.

It's Election Day.

The date was March 3, 2020, and I was to serve as a precinct officer for the first time ever. I was an experienced poll worker, but I was nervous about being in charge. Hundreds of people would be voting at my polling place and it was up to me to make sure things went according to plan. But I had turned my worries over to God before I fell asleep, confident that with His help the day would go smoothly.

Now, I was cowering in a beanbag chair in my musty, dimly lit basement, watching the weather report on my phone with increasing horror. Winds of 175 miles per hour were forming funnel clouds. Reports were coming in that a huge one had touched down a few miles west of where I live. Meteorologists were calling this storm cataclysmic.

Hugging my dog close, I prayed. *Please, God, wrap Your arms around those in the path of this storm. Give strength to the emergency responders. And guide me and all the other election workers as we perform our duties today.*

• • •

After what seemed like forever, the radar picture on my screen showed no more red. The tornado had finally worn itself out. Not knowing what might have happened aboveground in my neighborhood, I crept warily upstairs. My house was unscathed. Surveying my yard with a flashlight, I found only a few small tree limbs littering the lawn. Same for my neighbors' yards.

But when I turned on the TV, I learned that the tornado had strengthened to an EF4 intensity before touching down on the other side of town. As emergency workers arrived at that area, it was hard in the pitch-dark for them to know exactly what had happened and to locate those who needed help. Power lines were down, making the job especially difficult. It wasn't until the sun rose that the full extent of the devastation became clear. Houses flattened. Trees uprooted. Cars and trucks flipped upside down. Remnants of clothes and furniture and toys everywhere.

And there were so many victims. Some were only slightly injured, others badly hurt. Worst, of course, were the fatalities, several of them children.

In the midst of all the chaos and grief, we election workers had a job to do. A job that seemed overwhelming on a day like this. Guided by the secretary of state's office in Nashville, along with law enforcement officials and road crews, it was decided that eight of the county's twenty-two polling places couldn't open because of storm damage or blocked roads. Utilizing radio stations, social media, signs taped to precinct doors, and word of mouth, we spread the news that voters in the affected precincts would cast their ballots at the election office. Then we scrambled to put personnel in place, set up voting machines, and prepare ourselves to welcome who-knew-how-many voters.

I was asked to serve as a registrar, the person who greets voters and processes applications for a ballot. I wondered if I was emotionally prepared to handle it. Before I settled into my chair and logged on to my computer, I took a moment to pray. *Help me, Lord. Help me offer strength and hope to the hurting people who show up here today.*

The staff wondered out loud if any voters would come. How could people who'd lived through a tornado just a few hours earlier even remember that it was Election Day? And if they did remember, would they care? Voting seemed almost trivial in the aftermath of so much destruction and death. But when nine o'clock rolled around and the administrator of elections unlocked the front door, she saw a line of people stretching the entire length of the sidewalk and into the parking lot. Hour after hour, in they came to vote. Most looked shell-shocked. Many were in tears. Some of those who came to my counter poured out their stories.

"My house is gone," one of them said. "Completely gone."

"My dogs are missing," another told me.

"My next-door neighbor didn't make it to her basement in time," one woman said as tears streamed down her cheeks. "They found her body an hour ago."

And I would offer a weak smile and wipe tears from my own cheeks and say I was so, so sorry for their suffering and so, so glad that they'd come to vote. "What made you show up here today?" I asked one man who seemed eager to talk.

He shrugged. "Because it's patriotic, I guess," he said. "And it's normal. In a day when nothing's like it's supposed to be, at least I could cast my ballot."

For ten solid hours, my coworkers and I listened to one heartbreaking story after another. We clasped hands with voters and passed out tissues and offered words of sympathy and support. *How could this ever be OK?* I wondered. *How could this community ever heal?*

• • •

I got answers when I walked outside to the parking lot during a late afternoon break. Trees that had been bare for months were just beginning to show new green leaves. Yellow dandelions smiled up from the still-brown grass. And in the shallow pond at the far end of the parking lot, spring peepers—tiny chorus frogs whose melodic evening chirping is a sure sign that winter won't be around much longer—were tuning up to serenade anyone who would listen.

I sank onto a bench near the front door and watched people greet each other as they emerged from their cars. I saw them shake hands and hug one another so tight it seemed they might not ever let go.

I listened as they shared stories from that terrible, terrible morning. Stories of trauma and tragedy. But stories of triumph too. I listened as they prayed together and as they promised to be there for each other. Nineteen people in my county were killed in that tornado. Entire neighborhoods and several businesses were wiped out. But on that unforgettable Election Day, I knew beyond a shadow of a doubt that our community would heal and rebuild and prosper. We were strong people. We were resilient people. We were faith-filled people.

And I was right. Even in the face of a global pandemic that became all too real not long after that fateful day, we picked ourselves up, dusted ourselves off, and forged ahead, standing always on the promises of God.

Prayer for a Hope-Filled Life

Heavenly Father, grant me strength to offer help to the helpless and hope to the hopeless, whatever the circumstances and in whatever way I can.

Yet I still dare to hope when I remember this: The faithful love of the LORD never ends! His mercies never cease. Great is his faithfulness; his mercies begin afresh each morning.

Lamentations 3:21–23 (NLT)

IT CAN ALL CHANGE IN A DAY

By Michelle Stiffler

IT WAS SPRING WHEN my husband was offered a job promotion to manage his company's western division. We lived in Virginia, across the country from the western states, so he was offered two options: He could work remotely from Virginia or he could accept the company's offer of a small stipend for our family to move to Arizona.

We discussed the offer and found ourselves leaning toward the move, which seemed ridiculous at first. Why not stay put, enjoy the solid roots and relationships we'd established over a decade? We loved our community, and my family was just a few miles away. Life was good. Despite this, we'd often entertained a move to a warmer climate. A job change made it seem possible, or at least, more rational. In the fall, each of our four children would enter school years that made the timing seem right for our family. If there was ever a good time to undertake a cross-country move, we were in that window of time. After much prayer, we both agreed God had opened the door for a move, and even though many details had to fall into place, we'd trust Him to orchestrate our new adventure.

A flurry of closet clearing, box packing, and deep cleaning ensued. We painted walls and made repairs, manicured the yard, and added inviting touches to the house that had long been home. Selling the house was the first step, and without that crucial step, there was no means for securing our new house in our new town. Consequently, my biggest worry and most frequent prayer was about selling the house. If it sold quickly, we could move mid-summer, just in time for the kids to start school. My mental scenario had us creating a new life before fall.

That's not how things played out, though. After listing our home, we had a handful of showings, but no offers. I often reminded God about the perfect order I'd imagined for our move. He wasn't following the time line, and to make matters more confusing, adversity came. The day my husband flew to Arizona for training, sickness came to our home and plagued all but one of my children for a month. Soon after everyone was well again, the fringes of a hurricane hit our area and took down our power lines. For the next nine days, we went about our daily routine with the assistance of a portable generator.

• • •

Life went on. I re-enrolled my children for school in Virginia, bracing as the unpleasant office assistant quipped, "I thought you were moving." Many people had asked about our move over the summer. I appreciated the sincere questions from people who cared, but when the questions were cynical, they only added to my shame. "We're moving," I assured the office assistant, forcing a smile. "Things haven't gone according to plan."

My frequent prayer had become a series of questions: *God, why are You waiting? Why can't You see the perfect time line I imagined? Why are You allowing it to slip by?* I'd experienced times before when God seemed silent. This time, He seemed absent.

Soon after our electricity returned, I made chili and baked brownies. Comfort food has always established a sense of normalcy for my family. The cool September air breezed in through the windows as we gathered around the table, joyful and grateful. Cleaning up afterward, I paused to enjoy the setting sun's last rays on changing leaves. It was a hopeful scene. *I* was hopeful. But then I noticed a bubbling puddle in the yard, right above the septic tank. The following day, a septic company dug up our yard and sent us a bill.

It'd been a perilous couple of months, and I was utterly drained. Relentlessly, I'd spoken hope to my discouraged family, reminding them—and myself—we could brave the trials and that God had a plan. And I knew in my heart that He did, but I was frustrated. His plans weren't working out very well. It seemed like my life was on hold with no end in sight. I'd been so confident in the spring that the Lord was directing us to move. Had I been wrong?

One October morning, I scheduled coffee with a friend. As I was driving to meet her, the clouds let loose as if they'd been storing rain past their capacity. Drenched, chilled to the bone, and completely unable to fake it anymore, I ordered my favorite coffee and lamented to my friend. She listened, then responded with wisdom that made sense to both of us: Call off the move. My husband was already working remotely from a makeshift office in our laundry room. The kids were back in school. I still had my part-time job. We had a house that wasn't under contract, nor were we under contract to buy another home elsewhere. We could stay put.

I drove home and marched into the laundry room with a directness that reminded me of my younger self. "Call it off," I told my husband. He turned to meet my gaze and I continued, "This move isn't working and the whole process has been awful. Tell your boss we're not moving."

Calmly, my husband replied, "I can't do that."

I pushed. "You can't, or you won't?"

My husband's answer was steady and clear. "I *won't* do that."

He reminded me how we'd sensed the move was God's plan, how God had continued to assure us over the months, even in the hardships we'd recently endured. We discussed other options, made a phone call to a rental agent, and within a few days, prospective renters toured our home and signed a rental agreement. It was the first step I hadn't anticipated and we could finally move forward. My husband returned to Arizona to find our new home and I stayed back with the kids. We'd all move in December, after school let out for the year. It was a different plan from the original, but it was the final plan.

• • •

A month before moving day, boxes were stacked to the ceiling, but our new home had yet to be found. The summer's booming housing market had come to a halt and there were little to no homes available. It seemed ironic that finding a new home was now our biggest obstacle, especially when we were so close! Unable to sleep, I sat in the family room with my Bible. I'd read the story of Noah more times than I could count, but this time, his story resonated. Noah was a man willing to obey God's leading, willing to prepare for something he'd never seen and couldn't imagine. Noah waited and obeyed for one hundred years; I'd waited only five months. Why was my faith so fragile?

I prayed a tired prayer, and there in the dark, I heard God whisper: "It can all change in a day." I was hesitant to accept this idea, but wasn't it true? Throughout each trial we'd encountered, I'd certainly seen it. The kids were sick for weeks on end, then one day, they were well. Our electricity was out for what seemed an eternity, then one day, the power came back on. We waited for house showings and a contract, then one day, we had a signed rental agreement. At other moments in my life, I'd weathered various challenges that stretched long, until one day, each situation changed. I went to bed that night knowing our big change would come and God would work it out in His perfect timing. I would trust him.

Things did change the next day. A house beyond our dreams appeared on the market and a few days before Christmas, we filled it with furniture and boxes and began creating our new life. A decade later, the promise God whispered to me that November night is still my hope mindset. When I'm facing adversity that won't budge, I remind myself that God is faithful, and things can change in a day.

Prayer for a Hope-Filled Life

Lord, in times of waiting, remind me to put my hope in You by trusting that change is in Your hands and will happen in Your time.

**Take delight in the Lord,
and he will give you the desires
of your heart.**

Psalm 37:4 (NIV)

THE DESIRE OF MY HEART

By Maureen Miller

THE PASSAGE FROM Psalm 37 pierced my heart, and I wondered what it meant. "Lord, is this verse particular to my longing? If so, show me what to do with these words."

For several years, I'd been waiting—white-knuckling my dream for a child. I hardly knew how to pray, afraid God's answer would be no.

But when I read in the Psalms that God gives us the desires of our hearts, my attention perked up. Was God speaking specifically to me?

Many others had offered messages. Doctors at the University of Kentucky had deemed me infertile, the result of polycystic ovary disease. Despite several rounds of fertility medications, egg harvesting, and painful procedures, I didn't conceive. "Void a miracle, you'll never have children biologically." That's what I'd been told.

Pastors, too, spoke to my situation. "God has a plan for your life. Trust Him." But while I knew this, these words alone weren't what I longed to hear.

Truth be told, what I wanted someone to say was, "God has children in your future." And with this newly discovered Bible verse, I hoped the Psalmist's message spoke about my specific longing.

My husband, Bill, was kind to encourage. "There are still options, so try not to worry." But I knew. He, too, longed for children—not simply to satisfy the desires of my heart but his as well.

Still, with so many friends having babies, I'd begun battling despair, dreading being invited to one more baby shower or receiving another birth announcement in the mail. Each stung, salt in my wound.

I read the passage again, pondering each word. If God promised to give me the desires of my heart, what was I to do? The answer was clear. I was to delight in Him.

Perhaps it was simply being friends with God—talking to and listening to one another, which is prayer. Reading His words. Sitting in His presence.

At the very least, I figured doing this would deepen our relationship, and what was the harm in that? If children weren't part of His plan for my life, maybe He'd at least change my desires so they better matched whatever His plan happened to be.

This new perspective enabled me to petition differently. Rather than clutching my dreams for a child with closed fists, I began to loosen my grasp, praying instead with hands up and open—my dreams lifted to the Lord. If a child wasn't to be mine, then surely He would mercifully remove my desire, replacing it with something better, though it was difficult to imagine what that could be.

• • •

Change didn't happen all at once. It took time, but as I persisted, God filled my heart with peace—replacing fear with a hope that He knew best.

Years passed. I continued journeying with Jesus, discovering that, through all life's seasons, He really was my best friend.

One day during my quiet time, I read a story about Abraham and Sarah entertaining three visitors. One of their guests told Abraham, "I will surely return to you about this time next year, and Sarah your wife will have a son" (Genesis 18:10, NIV).

These words struck me, and I wondered, *Lord, are You saying something? Do You mean, by this time next year, I'll be like Sarah and give Bill a son?*

As I sat in that quiet space trying to hear God's heart, He reminded me. Mother's Day—a holiday that, even after all the healing, still brought a bit of heartache—had recently come and gone. Like years past, I'd again felt that familiar tug of longing. It was as if the Lord whispered, "I know your heart's desire. Don't you think I'd have taken it away—replaced it—if it weren't part of My plan? Rest in knowing it is."

And that day was a turning point. When I rose from my chair, I did so with a firm belief. Not only was God saying yes to my desire to be a mom, He'd spoken specifically about the timing. Like the promise given in this Old Testament passage, I believed that, at about the same time the following year, we, too, would have a child.

In the course of the next 365 days, we were indeed like Abraham and Sarah. Like these ancient sojourners, we moved too. I was soon teaching, and Bill began the first year of his medical residency in South Carolina.

The weeks and months passed. I couldn't help but wonder what would happen. Would I soon discover I was pregnant? The window to actually have a child in the time spoken about the previous year had closed. Was there something I'd not understood?

A friend with whom I'd confided asked, "What do you think God meant?"

And I answered with confidence. "I don't know. But I do know this—He who promised is faithful. I may be in heaven before I understand this mystery, but I believe God said it, and I'll keep walking with hope, by faith, in His word."

Bill and I decided to wait the remaining months of 1997 to see what God might do, but come the new year, we were determined to move ahead. Perhaps our family would grow through the miracle of adoption.

The year came to an end. On Friday, January 2, I had an appointment with a woman who ran an adoption ministry in our community. Over the course of several hours, we shared our stories.

By the time I left, though it was dark outside, a flame was lit within me. Over the next couple of weeks, Bill and I worked to prepare a room for a child as well as to create a portfolio for prospective birth mothers, filled with family photographs and letters from each of us, sharing more about our desire for a family.

We began to pray, too, for the women who'd read our words, asking God to guide and protect each one. To protect each unborn baby also, and to bring a child—God's chosen child for us—to our waiting arms in His perfect time.

• • •

Several weeks after that initial meeting, we received the call we'd been hoping for. "There's a young birth mom—a student at the University of South Carolina. She's seen your portfolio and wants to meet you. You should know, she's in her last trimester, due in early February."

The arrangements were made for us to visit in the office of an adoption attorney in Columbia. As we stepped through the door, we saw her. A teenager wearing a baggy sweatshirt and loose-fitted pants stood when we entered. Her bangs hung low, covering fearful eyes.

"Allow me to introduce everyone," the attorney said. "Cindy, this is Bill and Maureen Miller." Turning to us, "I'd like you to meet Cindy. Cindy Abrams."

Guiding us to a conference room, he invited us to sit. The attorney then stood by the door. "I'll leave you alone to get to know one another. Just pop your head out when you're ready, and we'll discuss the possibility of moving forward."

With that, strangers—a childless couple and a pregnant young woman—remained. Painfully shy, Cindy fixed her gaze on her hands clasped in front of her, pressed hard against the tabletop, knuckles white like mine once were.

Bill cleared his throat. "So you're a student. What are you studying?"

Looking up, her eyes locked with mine for a moment before shifting her attention to Bill. "Yes, sir. I'm...I'm a freshman." She paused. "I've...I've always dreamed of being a lawyer."

My first thought—*She's dreamed too. That's something we have in common.*

Irony struck and I spoke, "Oh, that's wonderful." Rising emotion threatened to hijack my words, and I, too, cleared my throat.

After a beat of silence, I said, "Sometimes things happen that we don't plan, and sometimes things don't happen that we've hoped for." Bill squeezed my hand under the conference table, giving me what I needed to continue, "Do you believe God can work everything out, making good of that which might seem like a mistake? A mess even?"

Her eyes pooled, but the young woman's courageous answer held the promise my heart needed. "Yes. Yes, I do."

Our son was born less than two weeks later. Dorian Samuel, whose name means "gracious gift of God for whom I prayed," entered the world in God's perfect time on February 3, 1998.

It wasn't until several months later that Cindy confirmed what I already believed. She'd conceived right around Mother's Day the year before—our son's life beginning in the womb exactly when God promised through the passage in Genesis 18.

Only it wasn't me giving my husband a child. Rather, it was another. Specifically, God used a young birth mom to fulfill the desires of my heart when Cindy gave us her son.

Prayer for a Hope-Filled Life

Kind Father, thank You for Your Word, which is a lamp for my path in all life's dark places. Help me trust You, even when I don't understand—believing You'll fulfill the desires of my heart by first planting the seeds of Your dreams in my soul. Amen.

**Before they call I will answer;
while they are still speaking
I will hear.**

Isaiah 65:24 (NIV)

HAVE YOU EVER picked up the phone to call someone, only to hear a hesitant "Hello?"—the telephone not having even rung on your end. How about opening the front door to find a friend standing on the welcome mat, hand raised to knock?

It's a wonderful, though at times unsettling, surprise to discover our desires are taken care of prior to voicing them. We don't plan these phenomena. We can't. When they do occur, we might think they are a fluke. But believers know they are messages from God.

If you're like me, you've sent prayers heavenward countless times, begging for rescue or a solution to a problem. God never fails to respond with a "yes," "no," "maybe later," or better yet, "I have something else in mind." No matter what His answer is, He is steadfast to listen for our calls.

Almost as often, God astonishes us, by answering our requests before we've made them or have even recognized our need. When this has happened to me,

I've folded my hands and bowed my head, awed by His wisdom.

How does God know what we need? Even more importantly, how do we know God is listening, even when our pleas are silent? The Bible tells us He is ever present in our lives. In the midst of billions of people, He sees and loves each of us as a treasured individual. He waits for us to call to Him in praise. He listens as we cry out in fear or sorrow. And often, like the loving Father He is, He'll step in to help even before we realize it's necessary.

God knows us. He stood witness as we grew in the womb and watched in delight as we gasped our first breaths. He walks alongside us, directing and refining our lives' paths. When we are hurt, He holds us close, and when we triumph, His joy surpasses ours. And He'll be there, arms spread wide, when we've breathed our last breath. He has promised this to be true, and we can trust Him to see, to hear, to know, and to answer even the unspoken prayer.

He will answer our every call.

—Heidi Gaul

The righteous will flourish like a palm tree, they will grow like a cedar of Lebanon; planted in the house of the LORD, they will flourish in the courts of our God. They will still bear fruit in old age, they will stay fresh and green.

Psalm 92:12–14 (NIV)

FLOURISH LIKE A PALM TREE

By Mindy Baker

WHEN MY FIRST BABY was born, I remember how much I snuggled, cuddled, rocked, and cradled my precious newborn infant, feeling very much in awe of this tiny bundle that God had entrusted to me. She was a miracle of life, and in my eyes, perfect in every way. However, despite all the wonder and deep love that I felt for her, I can also vividly remember the shock this life change was to my personal identity.

My husband and I had made the commitment that I would quit my job teaching in the public school and become a stay-at-home mom, focused on raising our kids. Although I believe our faith led us to this decision, I experienced a deep struggle in my heart and mind trying to find my self-worth in my new role as a mother. I have to admit that a daily routine of nursing the baby, changing her diapers, and doing chores around the house left me wondering why I had ever thought this was a good idea.

The transition from a life of lesson planning and a busy classroom to an empty house with only an infant for company was very isolating. I felt alone. The enemy of my soul pounced on this weakness and whispered, "You are useless. You have no purpose."

Looking back, I can see that I fell into this trap because I didn't realize how much I was defining my self-worth by my role as a teacher. Without that title, I falsely believed I didn't have any value. I had yet to discover that I didn't need to earn God's favor, nor did I need to achieve success in the workplace to be worthy of His love.

It took a while, but over time I developed some friendships with women who were also choosing to stay at home to raise their children. I got involved in a Bible study at a local church and met other young moms through activities that my kids were involved in. There were play dates, picnics in the park, church events, and sports teams, and countless other ways that my life intersected with moms who were raising kids the same ages as mine. We shared our lives and our hearts with one another and we prayed for one another. Gradually, "being a mom" became my identity, a new way of defining myself and a new way of life. Instead of resenting my role as mom, I felt like I was flourishing in it.

• • •

Fast-forward years later to the present. Now that my last child has left for college, I am faced with an empty nest. The identity crisis has returned, but in reverse. Yes, I am still a "mom," but my role has changed dramatically. Because my kids are older, I am no longer needed in the same way as I have been for the past twenty-three years. Longing for the past instead of enjoying the current season has now become a very real mental battle.

I miss being the "minivan taxi driver." My grocery cart seems strangely empty when it is void of kid-friendly snacks. Going to the zoo, the spray park, or the children's museum are no longer appointments on my calendar. Once again, I am struggling to find my self-worth, and the enemy of my soul is back with his same tactic, whispering, "You are useless. You have no purpose."

Just when my self-worth reached its lowest point, God used Scripture to show me a new way. It happened not too long ago, when our family traveled south for a beach vacation. I noticed how different it felt to travel as a family when our three kids were eighteen and older. Don't get me wrong, I cherished the experience, but I definitely noticed the change. To be honest, I felt old and not needed. I had always been the one to organize the itinerary and help everyone make sure they had everything for the day. Now we were five grown adults, each with different ideas of how the vacation should go. And my organizational reminders seemed like nothing more than nagging.

One morning during the trip, I woke up early and went to the beach to pray. I poured out my heart to the Lord about the emotions I was feeling. Surrounded by the lapping water and vibrant palm trees, God used Psalm 92:12–14 to breathe hope into my spirit. As I read the verses, He seemed to tenderly whisper, "I am not done using you." Then He lovingly reminded me that He has prepared good work for me to do no matter my age. He has called me to bear fruit for His Kingdom. If I stay in His Word and abide in Him, I will stay as fresh and green as the palm trees that surrounded me on the beach no matter my circumstances.

That morning, those verses helped me to feel refreshed and hopeful, and open to new possibilities. The rest of our trip wasn't perfectly harmonious, but we did relax and soak up the sun, rented bikes and tried parasailing, and made some wonderful memories that I will forever cherish.

I carried home the hope God breathed into my heart that morning on the beach, and I have referred back to those verses many times in moments of weakness. God has also used other scriptures to remind me that my worth is not defined by what I do but is instead rooted in the fact that I am His child. Even if I never do another act of service or never hold another job, He will still value and cherish me because I am His creation. However, it is because of His great love for me that I am motivated to serve Him and bear fruit for His Kingdom.

• • •

As the year has progressed with all three kids now in either college or grad school, I have continued to ask God to open my eyes to new opportunities and new possibilities. He has answered with little sprigs of opportunity popping up. There was a family in need at our church, and I volunteered to babysit. I started a Bible study with a few young women in their twenties. I am finding that if I listen to His voice and follow His leading, He will use me in this new season of my life with the people who are in my sphere of influence.

A mentor friend also recently reminded me that couples normally spend more time together *after* their kids have left the nest than when they are together raising their kids. Learning this caused me to pause and reflect on my marriage. What can my spouse and I do together for the Kingdom of God? Are there people around us whom we can minister to together? The answer is a resounding, "Yes!"

I pray that my heart stays filled with God's hope, that my eyes and heart will remain open to the new opportunities He sets in my path, and that I will flourish like a palm tree.

Prayer for a Hope-Filled Life

Lord, breathe new hope into my heart for my future. Open my eyes to the good work You have prepared for me to do. Keep me fresh and green for Your service.

Instead, they were longing for a better country—a heavenly one. Therefore God is not ashamed to be called their God, for he has prepared a city for them.

Hebrews 11:16 (NIV)

BACK TO THIS PLACE

By Cathy Bryant

MY FAMILY'S HISTORY IS deeply rooted in Central Texas. Many of my ancestors immigrated to America in the early 1800s and settled in the heart of Texas. The farm my grandparents owned and operated had been passed down to them from my great-great-grandparents, and the deed to the land included the name of the first governor of Texas.

Though my childhood had its fair share of difficulties, I have many fond memories of growing up in the Texas Hill Country. So I was beyond elated when early in my marriage and while our two sons were little, my husband landed a teaching position in the area.

Living back in the place so embedded in my heart and soul was like living in the town of Mayberry from *The Andy Griffith Show*, with tree-lined streets, cozy neighborhoods, a close-knit community, and more. Since both our boys were young when we moved, it quickly became the only home they remembered. Highly involved in both the church and community, we hoped we could make our little town in Central Texas our earthly forever home.

But God had other plans.

• • •

Seven years later, my husband and I both felt the Lord calling us into full-time music ministry. At the time, we weren't sure exactly what that would entail, but we both had a feeling it involved music evangelism and leading music at revivals in various churches around the country. One Sunday morning we both walked to the front of our church during the invitation to make our decision public. The next day, each of us told our respective campus principals that we were resigning our teaching positions, effective at the end of the school year.

It was an exciting time but also very stressful. My personality leans toward anxiety, fear, and worry, three foes I've battled my entire life. What had we been thinking? We had two young children, our paychecks would stop in August, and we had absolutely no job prospects. Despite our confusion, we clung to our calling, trusting the Lord to work it out for us.

And He did.

A church at which my husband had previously served as a bi-vocational music minister called us to do the music for their upcoming revival meeting. With our boys now in school and the revival only lasting a week, some friends offered to keep our children. Soon after that, a second church called, having been referred by the first church. The person this church had lined up for the music for their revival services had backed out. They asked us to fill in at the last minute, which we were happy to do. Once more, our friends offered to keep our kids. This revival was even closer, and we were so grateful that the Lord was providing in so many ways. Perhaps His plan was to let us stay in the place we loved, but how could we continue to leave our children behind, even with great friends?

That second revival service was near the end of September, the time at which we would be receiving our paychecks had we continued to teach. The love offering we received from that revival was almost exactly what our combined checks would have totaled.

There was absolutely no doubt in our minds that God was providentially meeting our needs and directing our course. Everything seemed to be heading in the direction we had imagined our new lives to look like. My main concern was for our two young sons. Leaving them with friends or family members was not a long-term solution. I began the process of checking into homeschooling so that the boys could travel with us.

But again, God had plans other than what we expected. That second church called a week later, asking my husband to come in to interview as their new music minister.

• • •

At first I was overjoyed at the prospect of a sure job and steady income. Then reality hit.

This wasn't what I thought I signed up for. The plan was to partner with my husband as music evangelists, not to be the wife of a church minister. Even more devastating was the realization that we would be leaving the place we all loved, the place we had hoped to settle down in for the rest of our earthly lives.

My husband and I had multiple discussions about the situation and prayed about it, both together and individually. We also enlisted others to pray on our behalf.

Deep in my heart, after struggling in prayer over the matter, I knew the Lord was once again providing and that this move was His plan for us. Determined to make the best of the situation and stay true to God's leading, I shoved my heartbreak aside and dived into the preparations for getting us moved. Then one night, returning home from a goodbye party hosted by our close friends, I could no longer contain my tears.

God, please don't make us leave. This is our home, a place we love, the only home our boys know. Please don't rip us away from our friends and family.

The next morning, I read the story of Jacob in Genesis 28:15. My heart still ached from the night before. I came to the point of the story where God told Jacob that He would bring him back to his homeland of Canaan, the place He had given to Jacob's forefathers, Abraham and Isaac.

A knot formed in my throat and a flicker of hope ignited in my chest. I knew that promise was specifically given to Jacob, but under our current circumstances, it also felt as though the Lord was comforting and encouraging me in my heartbreak.

Was it possible that He would one day bring us back to our beloved Central Texas?

Over the next several days, I held on to that promise as we packed boxes, loaded them on the moving truck, and headed to our new location. I also tucked the promise in my heart as we unpacked and started life in a new town and a new line of work. As a mother, my primary concern was for our boys and making sure they adjusted well to the changes. I never dreamed I would be the one to struggle with our new circumstances.

• • •

There were days when the promise seemed impossible, days when I wanted to pack up the truck and move back, days when I felt alone and abandoned. Learning to cope with the many unwritten rules laid on me as the wife of a church staff member was challenging to say the least. Having to hold my tongue while at the receiving end of some pretty hurtful words placed wounds in my heart that still plague me from time to time. I cried out to the Lord more often than not. Each time, that promise came to mind, the Lord's way of carrying me through my very real battle with the enemy.

I eventually reached a place of acceptance with my husband's work. We served in a total of four churches in the years that followed, and I have sweet friends and wonderful memories from each place. But still my heart longed for the place of my birth, the place where three generations of my ancestors had been born and lived and passed on to be with the Lord. I still waited for that promise from the Lord to be fulfilled.

It finally happened, around twenty-five years later, when we moved back to the area to be close to my mom, who was aging and in declining health. We began to discuss and pray through the possibility. Doors had already started closing in the place we lived. Promises made in a job situation were revoked without reason. Relationships with friends and family in the area had changed due to unforeseeable circumstances. We began to do online research for the possibility of selling our house. In what can only be described as a miracle, we had an offer within twelve hours, with two other potential buyers waiting right behind. Again, the Lord was moving, opening some doors and closing others.

Going on five years now, we have enjoyed being back in the place so rich in my family history. As I look back over the journey that took us away and brought us back again, I can't help but give thanks to the Lord for fulfilling His promise to Jacob and me. I'm especially grateful for how the Lord used it all to draw me closer to Him and for comforting me time and again through His words of hope.

• • •

Life is far from perfect. Health concerns and financial conditions could mean another move. We can't know the future in the days we have left on the Earth. But because of God's faithfulness in the past, I know exactly where to turn for help. Had I not learned early in our journey to turn to Him in my struggles, would I have ever recognized Him as the source of all hope and comfort? Would I have been able to readily follow where He chooses to lead?

My journey has taught me that no matter how special Central Texas is to me, it is not my final home. And I am at peace with that, because even this place that I love so much is not worthy to be compared to the glory that awaits.

Prayer for a Hope-Filled Life

Father God, help me to always turn to You as my Father and Shepherd through the struggles of this earthly journey toward my eternal home.

For I hold you by your right hand—I, the Lord your God. And I say to you, "Don't be afraid. I am here to help you."

Isaiah 41:13 (NLT)

REMEMBER HOW FAR YOU'VE COME

By Laurie Davies

NO ONE SURVIVES spine surgery twice. At least that's what I told myself.

I had *just* completed the grueling work of physical therapy after a spinal fusion six months prior. Retraining my body to compensate for limited neck mobility in my mid-forties had taken me to the mat—literally, a flimsy blue mat in the physical therapy office—and three times a week I cried my way through humbling, simple exercises with elastic bands and foam rollers.

Over time, the tears and sweat that fell to that blue mat started to feel like an offering, a sacred physical and emotional outpouring of both belief and unbelief. On the mornings of PT, I would pick a "grind" Bible verse—something like "For the joy set before him, he endured the cross" (Hebrews 12:2, NIV) or "I can do all this through him who gives me strength" (Philippians 4:13, NIV)—and I would say it with each roll, rep, and tug. My faith grew as my strength grew. I began to imagine a healthy, full life again.

The morning I graduated from physical therapy, my team sent me off with high fives, a printout of home exercises, and a green resistance band I'd snapped in two during my third set of stretches one morning. You'd have thought I climbed Mount Everest that day. I was so happy I'd had the strength to break an overstretched, weakened green band.

My tech stuffed it into my file with a note to send it home with me at discharge. She scrawled this note across a prescription form and pinned it to the band: "Remember how far you've come."

It had been a full year of either pain leading up to surgery or pain recovering from it. My schedule had revolved around imaging tests, pain-relieving injections, doctor visits, and PT visits. Walking out the door from my physical therapy office that morning for the final time, I felt battle-tested and free. Physical reps built confidence in my body and scriptural reps bolstered my faith. Honestly, I had never felt stronger.

• • •

My stint being on cloud nine didn't last long. Two weeks later, I woke with familiar white-lightning nerve pain shooting down my arm. I had to grit my teeth just to get out of bed. The disabling pain in my neck and loss of feeling in my fingers told me what an MRI confirmed: I'd ruptured another disc in my spine.

I couldn't believe it. I had known that the disc below my fusion was weak, but I had been careful to continue my at-home strength training while avoiding heavy lifting. This timing seemed unfair. My suffering clock had just reset to zero.

This time, the pain was worse. Fear seeped deep into my thinking. A surgeon had rearranged the furniture in my neck once already, literally moving my esophagus and carotid artery to clear an operating path to my spine. I began to believe a self-imposed narrative that I couldn't survive the same surgery again. My mind became a runaway train that derailed into a spiral of false assumptions and fatalistic fears. I would not wake up from a second spinal fusion, I just knew it.

I set up a trust, which is a perfectly responsible thing for a woman in her forties to do—unless, as in my case, the trust is established because of a lack of real trust. Where had all my "grind" Bible verses gone? Was my hope pinned only to forward progress? Why was I certain my surgeon would not be able to put Humpty Dumpty together again?

By the morning of surgery, I lathered myself up into a full-blown state of despair. My surgeon sensed it the moment he walked into the pre-op room.

"How are you feeling?" he asked, wheeling his chair slowly to my bedside.

My bottom lip trembled. I surveyed the IV that tethered me to the side rail on my transport stretcher and looked down at the hospital gown that barely extended to my knees. The elastic of my surgical cap pressed the temples of my glasses uncomfortably against my head. This was no power position.

I thought about my son and how happy he'd been that I'd willed my way through his nine-hole golf tournament the day before. He'd birdied the third and shot for par on six and eight. Wracked with pain, I had set out to walk those nine holes even if it killed me.

"What if surgery kil—?"

No, I thought, exhaling sharply. His next golf match in three days was on my mind. His graduation in three years was something I didn't want to miss. He was still such a young kid. He needed his mom.

My surgeon took the hand that was unbridled by the IV—my right hand—and said, "Listen to me. I fix spines like you fix punctuation. I'm good at what I do, just like you're good at what you do. I want you to feel strong today," he said.

And then he spoke the words that rocked me.

"Remember how far you've come."

• • •

Surely my PT tech's broken-green-band pep talk had not been recorded in my chart! Those were hype words. Hope words. God and my surgeon now had my full attention.

I sat up as straight as my angled bed would allow, wiped my tears, and settled into the promise God clearly wanted me to grasp. He'd been with me through every hard step and He wasn't going to let go of me now.

My paralyzing fear started to melt away. The flood of "grind verses" I'd memorized in a humble position on a blue mat came over me. Every rep *had* built muscle—and deepened my faith. I started to have the audacity to believe I would wake up in a couple of hours.

I wouldn't find out until later, but my surgeon navigated a tricky complication while I was on the table. The ruptured disc in my neck had scattered a few disc fragments into my nerve root. They had to be meticulously retrieved, piece by piece, both to alleviate my pain and to prevent the possibility that they might travel into my spinal fluid, causing possible paralysis or a fatal infection.

My husband later told me how nerve-wracking it was sitting in the waiting room for hours longer than expected. Every time the waiting room door opened, he looked for my surgeon. Finally, he just stopped reading the book he'd brought and stared at the door.

I woke up four hours later to these words: "Surgery was a success." I wiggled my fingers and toes to make sure.

My surgeon then talked for a minute to my husband, unsure if I was cognizant of the complications that had both prolonged the surgery and required an assistant surgeon to be called in. I tracked with some of the clinical terminology and I wanted him to talk to me.

"I'm awake and aware," I said, asking him to restate what he'd just said in simpler terms.

My surgeon turned to me.

"Remember the game Operation that you probably played when you were a kid?" he said. "I had to do that in your spine for a little while today. The good news is, I got all the pieces out and the red nose didn't buzz."

"Why didn't you say that in the first place?" I quipped.

"You *are* awake and aware," he joked, rising to leave.

"Thank you," I said, my voice breaking with gratitude. "You're right. You're good at fixing spines."

He smiled, opened the curtain, and left. My husband left to pick up our son so he could come hang out and watch the Phoenix Suns game in my hospital room that night. I sat alone with a cup of ice chips and my thoughts, grateful that when my hope seemed thin, the God of all hope used a well-timed word to remind me how sturdy His hand has always been.

I almost looked forward to hitting that flimsy blue mat to start building strength again. I made a mental note to add more weight to my faith training this time, challenging myself to find only Old Testament "grind verses" to get me through the endless physical reps that lay ahead.

And I remembered how far I'd come.

Prayer for a Hope-Filled Life

Lord, when fear paralyzes me, help me remember how far You've brought me and how fierce You are in protecting me.

For I am convinced that neither death nor life, neither angels nor demons, neither the present nor the future, nor any powers, neither height nor depth, nor anything else in all creation, will be able to separate us from the love of God that is in Christ Jesus our Lord.

Romans 8:38–39 (NIV)

LOVE. IT'S IN THE long, deep embraces we share with those dear to us. In a child's sticky hand offered during afternoon walks. In the sloppy kisses given by the family pet. Like faith and charity, love is an integral part of a believer's makeup.

There are probably as many ways to express affection as there are people in the world, each as individual and unique as snowflakes. And like them, the loving gestures we exchange seem fleeting when compared to eternity. Time, distance, health—even simple emotional fallibility—can wreak havoc on our closest relationships. We are human. Our level of tenderness, and its lack of constancy, sometimes reflects our temporary nature.

PROMISES TO YOUR LIFE

Yet there exists a love so strong as to be invincible, as we learn from this passage of Romans. Nothing can break its bond. All our forms of endearment are contained within its depth and power. And our greatest efforts to imitate or match this devotion only scratch the surface of its limitless expanse.

God's loving-kindness is in the smells, sounds, and tastes that we encounter and enjoy daily. We sense it in the gentle breeze caressing our faces on a hot summer's day. We witness it in the sublime beauty of the morning sun as it crests the horizon and in the budding of a perfect rose. We even feel God's love as He restores an estranged relationship.

The power of His love is also found in the pages of the Bible. Commitment to us is shown in God's selfless sacrifice of Jesus, and because of that sacrifice, our hope for life everlasting is born in His resurrection. Believers feel the heartbeat of eternal hope so deep and wide that like God's devotion, it spans time and space.

We can rely on this hope that possesses no start or finish, that fills our hearts and minds because it's built on the enduring, boundless foundation of love.

—Heidi Gaul

But those who hope in the LORD will renew their strength. They will soar on wings like eagles; they will run and not grow weary, they will walk and not be faint.

Isaiah 40:31 (NIV)

THE EAGLES ARE COMING

By Sarah Greek

IN J. R. R. TOLKIEN'S NOVEL *The Fellowship of the Ring*, the fictional character Haldir observes, "The world is indeed full of peril, and in it there are many dark places; but still there is much that is fair, and though in all lands love is now mingled with grief, it grows perhaps the greater." Tolkien's most famous works of fiction contain the rich fantasy world of elves, dwarves, hobbits, and humans, a landscape of beautiful imagery, and significant allegory. The heroes are brave and good, the trials they face seemingly impossible and insurmountable. Friendships are strong even in the darkest hour, and characters make real mistakes with real consequences. These are the sort of stories I get excited to introduce to my sons.

Somewhere in the middle of the pandemic lockdown, when I absolutely could not stand one more cartoon or another viewing of *Star Wars*, I introduced my boys to *The Hobbit*. It was an instant hit and became their next obsession for imaginative play. They found a cheap ring that had come from some carnival or vending machine and swore it made them invisible when they slipped it on. I knocked on their bedroom door one morning only to have them crack it open and shout, "No! Too many dwarves in here already!" and swiftly click it shut. Capes, wooden swords, and leather belt pouches became the dress at the breakfast table.

I was happy they had found an epic adventure game to play that kept them somewhat amused and busy while we waited out this unnerving and seemingly unending pause. Honestly, at that point, I don't know that I even cared what they played as long as I didn't have to be involved or settle too many disputes. I was empty and hollow and had nothing left to give.

• • •

The pandemic and all its consequences had effectively derailed all the plans we had been laying foundations for. Everything went sideways, and I felt the intense stress and sudden change rack my heart. I hate having zero sense of control, and this was that multiplied by a thousand. First, I was laid off, then my husband; the kids had no social time or contact with friends; I had no social time or contact with friends. We spent way too much time in our tiny hobbit hole of a home. It felt more like a goblin cave. All our savings for homestead projects and fun trips hemorrhaged to cover basic needs like heat and food.

I had always clung to the promise of God having plans for us, plans "not to harm you, plans to give you hope and a future" (Jeremiah 29:11, NIV). Now I wondered if those plans were all a mask. The truth being revealed by this trial was that we were all doomed. There was no hope and future, only death. This was not in fact a hero's journey to Mordor, the black, volcanic land Tolkien created; this was just a one-way ticket into the fire.

From the backyard one day, I overheard the boys play-acting a battle sequence with clashes of wooden swords and copious amounts of yelling and agonizing death sounds. (They could probably get jobs as sound effect engineers.) I heard my youngest shout in his best dwarfish accent, "There are too many enemies! We can never win now! We must run and hide!" And I thought to myself, *I hear ya, kid. I feel that in my bones.* My older boy scrambled up onto higher ground (I stopped telling them not to climb on the porch swing and the outbuilding and such somewhere around the time I started climbing the walls) and declared, "No, brother! Don't you remember how this ends? We fight on and on because we know the eagles are coming!"

Ah yes, the eagles.

Tolkien's imagery in his tales has been widely debated, with those seeking to confirm and to deny the parallels one can draw between his words and God's truths. I, for one, don't much mind what the intention was, just that God uses beautiful works such as this to speak if we have a mind to know. In the final battle scenes of these tales, all hope seems lost to the tired and worn heroes. Each blow dealt them seems like it will most certainly be the last they can take. And then it always gets worse! In more than one instance, the story has our battered heroes lifted out at the last minute, sometimes after suffering great losses, on the wings of giant eagles—summoned by a promise made to their wizard ally.

Now, I don't know that Tolkien's literal interpretation of "giant battle eagles" is what Scripture is actually promising us in Isaiah 40:31 (NIV). I contemplated this verse as saying we "will soar on wings as eagles and...will run and not grow weary." But I asked myself: How would I fight differently, face trials differently, live with hope differently if I actually believed that was a real possibility? If I remembered that the promise never says all *our* plans will survive, all *our* dreams, or even all our brethren?

• • •

The promise of hope says we will never be left to ruin and carnage. Even in the case of defeat, we are not left to enemy capture. The battle is not over if the eagles haven't come. We can hold on a little longer, fight one more round, expect one last surprise over the next horizon or with the next sunrise. The wise wizard companion of the little hobbits-turned-heroes says that it is not for us to decide what happens in our time. "All we have to decide is what to do with the time that is given us."

We all will find ourselves on many unexpected adventures, many of which we never asked to strike out on. We either walk those roads with capes and swords and the occasional second breakfast, or we allow despair to take root and crawl deep into the caverns of darkness where fear will have its way with us until we are unrecognizable. I'm going to wait for the eagles.

Prayer for a Hope-Filled Life

My God, be near me, travel beside me, fight before me, rest with me. Lift our heavy hearts with vibrant knowledge of the hope You offer.

You won't be able to say, "Here it is!" or "It's over there!" For the Kingdom of God is already among you.

Luke 17:21 (NLT)

LIGHT IN THE DARK SKY

By Darlene Kerr

THE LAST TWELVE MONTHS had been tough. Nearly everyone I love had been troubled with painful challenges, heartache, or illness. The nightly news had been persistently disturbing and often frightening. Life was often stressful, and human interactions around me were increasingly confrontational. I was spiraling downward into a pervasive state of discouragement and despair. Then I heard these words in my heart: "Kitt Peak."

Several years before, my sense of reality was altered when a view of God's creation unfolded before me. I exclaimed over my encounter with God's magnificence and His creative power during a stargazing program at Kitt Peak

National Observatory in southwest Arizona. The observatory is renowned for its twenty-four optical research telescopes located under one of the finest night skies in the world. The docent-led program included practicing with high-powered binoculars and star charts to find constellations, as well as opportunities to look through telescopes to see planets, galaxies, and other deep sky objects.

En route to the observatory, my husband and I carefully maneuvered the steep, winding road into the Quinlan Mountains located on the Tohono O'odham Indian Reservation. Dusk was imminent and all too soon we expected to be enveloped in complete darkness. There were no artificial lights on the ascent, and headlights were not permitted on the road as we snaked upward to the 6,877-foot Kitt Peak.

As we huddled with other participants outside in the chilly air, darkness deepened and the plethora of visible stars became stunning. We were told that the naked human eye can only hope to see between about 2,600 and 4,500 stars on any given night—and then only under perfect conditions. That night, atmospheric conditions were perfect. I experienced the full splendor of the night sky's celestial bodies and it seemed like billions were on display.

As I gazed upward, I was gobsmacked at the transformation. I've lived my life in urban settings with much light pollution and under my state's pervasive cloudy night skies. I didn't know what I was missing until my visit to Kitt Peak. Although my everyday view is limited to the few and brightest stars scattered across a blanket of darkness, I could bear witness to there being so much more.

• • •

And now, those words "Kitt Peak" spoke to my heart as I said my nighttime prayers. Particularly hard-hitting that day was the news of the death of someone for whom a slew of believers, including myself, had fervently prayed for healing. This strong believer was suddenly taken ill, endured multiple invasive medical interventions that ultimately failed, and died within four weeks. It's not that I expect every prayer for healing to result favorably, but I ardently hoped that I would see more that did. Once again, the evidence of God's authority seemed scant, and my prayers for the big things seemed fruitless.

My heart constricted as I recited my list of grievances—sickness, death, hatred, hunger, disasters, greed, violence… all abounding, seemingly uncensored by God. I prayed, "God, it feels like Satan and his kingdom are prevailing."

My mind flipped back the pages to that long-ago yet never-forgotten experience. It seemed a strange thought to have in the midst of wallowing in my skepticism. Or was it? Was God speaking to my heart with those two words, using a powerful memory to address my unbelief? After reflection, I believe He was saying to me, "Your view of the night sky is limited by clouds and city lights. But Kitt Peak showed you the reality of the night sky. My Kingdom's breakthroughs are more numerous than the stars you saw on Kitt Peak. And with each and every penetration of My Kingdom, there is more light, more hope, and more grace than you can ever see or absorb."

That night, God met me in the midst of my despair. I had lost sight of His promise that His Kingdom wins. I'd lost courage and faith as the mounting darkness of this broken world surrounded me.

I pondered the implications of this new insight. The breakthroughs of God's Kingdom are as numerous as the stars of the universe. Wow! What if I could fully see His Kingdom's breakthroughs? Wouldn't it be like the Kitt Peak experience? And then I saw it in my mind's eye—the billions of pinpricks of God's Kingdom ripping through the fabric of Satan's kingdom of darkness. This is what God knew I needed to see. "Thank You, Lord," I whispered.

• • •

Since that night, Kitt Peak has become my new code for God's Kingdom wins. "Kitt Peak," I remind myself when darkness seems to prevail. "Kitt Peak" whenever I see only a few instances of God's breakthroughs that never feel like enough. "Kitt Peak" after last week's visit to see my dearest friend, who is living with severe dementia.

The reality? God's promise that He wins does not obliterate the pain of the moments I live with when my heart breaks or when I face anxiety over devastating short- or long-term realities. Even so, when I grab onto His promise, I can reorient my perspective and denounce the despair. 2 Corinthians 4:18 (NLT) exhorts: "We don't look at the troubles we can see now; rather, we fix our gaze on things that cannot be seen. For the things we see now will soon be gone, but the things we cannot see will last forever." I can't hope to see all the breakthroughs of God's Kingdom, but I can believe His promise and rejoice in the evidence I can see.

As I dug deeper into Scripture, I realized that the Kingdom of God is mentioned more than eighty times in the New Testament. It was the key message of our Lord. Later, the Father sent the Holy Spirit to help us continue the work of Jesus in this world of darkness. Matthew 5:14 says believers are the light of the world like a city on a mountain, glowing in the night for all to see. And, when we are the light, we are partners in those breakthroughs. 1 John 5:4 (NLT) states, "Every child of God defeats this evil world, and we achieve this victory through our faith." This is our hope and encouragement.

I am grateful for the illuminating lesson I was given that evening during my prayer time. The memory of the stars I saw on Kitt Peak encourages my heart to believe that the breakthroughs of God's Kingdom are as uncounted as the stars in the heavens. I now draw strength and confidence in times when darkness tries to dominate my view. I can focus on the light and my brothers' and sisters' role in furthering God's Kingdom. He promises that His Kingdom wins, and we're part of that winning initiative. Darkness is on the run.

Prayer for a Hope-Filled Life

Lord, whatever the fears and heartaches that come my way today, I choose to cast my eyes toward Your Kingdom and say that no matter the shape of today's darkness, "God wins!"

The Lord will watch over your coming and going both now and forevermore.

Psalm 121:8 (NIV)

PROTECTION FOR THE PASSAGE

By Eryn Lynum

A TINY HUMMINGBIRD nervously peeked out from within my son's gentle grasp, its metallic gorget glimmering in the sunlight like a sequined scarf. We listened attentively to the ornithologist leading our three-day birding workshop in the Rocky Mountains. He explained the history and processes of bird banding as birds flitted overhead among the tree canopy. As he carefully transferred the tiny bird from my son's hands to his, our teacher told us that a hummingbird's legs are so thin they cannot walk or hop like other birds. As he explained this, he attached a nearly weightless metal band around the hummingbird's leg with incredible precision and care. After jotting down the microscopic numbers engraved on the band in his notebook, he released the bird, and it safely flew away.

Throughout the morning, as more hummingbirds, along with towhees, sparrows, finches, and warblers, flew in and out of the bird-banding site, we learned that scientists have been carefully banding birds and tracking their migration journeys since the early 1900s. More than six million birds have been banded. Of those six million, one million have been reencountered, helping scientists learn more about where and why certain birds travel and how successful they are on their impressive journeys.

My thoughts drifted from the birds flitting about to my firstborn, ten years old, sitting on a bench listening intently. He wrote an essay and proposal and received a grant to participate in this intensive birding workshop and to bring me along as his very willing chaperone. When we arrived at our cabin in the mountains, I'd given him a new pair of binoculars and an illustrated bird book to document his sightings. Over the weekend, he would record twenty-eight species of birds as we wandered through God's glorious mountains.

• • •

It was May, and many birds were deep into their migration journeys. I considered my son on his own passage into adolescence. What might his own journey ahead hold? So many things have changed since I was his age. How many times have I pleaded with God for my son's mental, physical, and spiritual safety as I watch an ever-shifting world? Raising him and his three younger siblings constantly pressures my faith. I must daily accept that there are so many details of life I cannot orchestrate or manipulate and trust God that whatever is outside my control is entirely within His authority.

I was reminded of this truth that morning when the news brought a devastating report of another tragedy. Children my son's age lost their lives. My heart ached for their grieving parents. Fear seeped into my soul as I stared into the fragility of life. Where is hope in all of this? My son had come out of his room to find me at the kitchen table in our cabin, teary-eyed and in prayer. I cautiously explained the situation to him. He asked me why tragedies happen. I told him that because this world is broken by sin, evil is inside of people.

While I cannot shelter him from everything in the world, I can guide him to God's promise of ultimate protection. I can remind him of King David's prayer in Psalm 140:4 (NIV), "Keep me safe, LORD, from the hands of the wicked; protect me from the violent, who devise ways to trip my feet." I reminded my son, "The important thing is that we choose to focus on all that is good, true, and lovely." With that in mind, we set out on another day of attuning our ears to birdsong and spotting God's goodness in creation.

Later that morning, it was my turn to help at the bird-banding station. Our instructor carefully situated a pine siskin—a finch with subtle yellow highlights—into my grasp, then turned back to his station to prepare the metal band. Admiring the tiny bird, I wondered where his journey would take him and if he might be encountered by another ornithologist along the way. Would the numbers on his metal bracelet be recorded in another notebook, then into a digital record, and help scientists further understand how these birds manage their migrations? Would a delay in his journey allude to what bird-watchers call a "fallout," or emergency stop, because of an imminent threat?

• • •

I have experienced fallouts in my life. I can be so fixated on my destination that I risk proceeding when the way is unsafe. Yet God is teaching me to slow down and seek His refuge in Psalm 57:1 (NIV): "Have mercy on me, my God, have mercy on me, for in you I take refuge. I will take refuge in the shadow of your wings until the disaster has passed."

Like a bird stopping prematurely to wait out an unexpected storm, I can discern dangers along my way with God's help. He invites me into His sanctuary to restore and strengthen me for the rest of the journey.

We encountered vivid reminders of God's refuge and strength throughout our bird-watching weekend. An American redstart caught my attention on the lakeshore with his contrasting neon orange and onyx feathers. The small, round songbird hopped along the rocky beach, unaware of my fixation. I had never seen one before and was grateful for this unique opportunity to spot him along his migration path. He belongs to the family of warblers. And perhaps never more than when studying warblers have I grasped God's tender care and faithful guidance.

I often think of the American redstart's cousin, the black-poll warbler, who takes an astonishing nonstop 2,500-mile flight over the Atlantic Ocean each autumn. Like the black-poll warbler's migration, the path before me can feel insurmountable. In my marriage, motherhood, health, career, ministry, and faith, I can feel like a tiny bird embarking on an overwhelming journey. Yet, how these birds prepare for their voyages draws my attention to God's provision. Before a black-poll warbler's flight commences, he carefully prepares with a time of rest and fueling up. He doubles his weight to make it across the Atlantic. How might I likewise, before beginning a new venture, set aside time to rest and fill up on God's goodness, power, and wisdom to sustain me when my resolve wanes?

• • •

It's not only a bird's preparations but also how it navigates the skies that remind me of God's protection. On our third and final morning of birding, our necks were strained and sore from looking up for three days. Yet as we made our way to the parking lot after our final hike, another new-to-me bird demanded my attention, and I craned my neck. The red-naped sapsucker pecked meticulously at tree branches getting at the insects inside the bark. Here was another bird we'd encountered on his sojourn. I wondered if it stopped in this valley along each seasonal passage.

Scientists and bird-watchers have long marveled at how such tiny creatures navigate sprawling stretches of sky.

Researchers discovered that birds have a protein in their eyes that enables them to see the earth's magnetic field, which they use as a directional beacon. In addition, scientists believe that songbirds can sense the magnetic field along with polarized light and can also use stars as a map at night. All of these provide a constant compass to guide them along the way.

When evil punctuates the news, tragedy strikes, or life's hardships stunt or stop my progress, I become disoriented. I quickly lose sight of the vision God has called me to. Yet much like birds use God's creation to find their way, I have God's Word and Holy Spirit to direct my paths—even through the dark. When I misstep or stumble, I can trust God's promise in Isaiah 30:21 (NIV): "Whether you turn to the right or to the left, your ears will hear a voice behind you, saying, 'This is the way; walk in it.'" He is protecting my course.

Each bird we'd carefully held, banded, and recorded in our birding books over the weekend were beautiful reminders of God's promise of protection. I heard a melody of deliverance and delight in each bird's song. Memorizing their chorus, I can pray with the Psalmist in Psalm 119:133 (ESV), "Keep steady my steps according to your promise."

Prayer for a Hope-Filled Life

Dear Lord, I rest secure in Your guidance and protection. When the way ahead is uncertain, I take shelter in Your refuge, and in Your strength I press on.

And God is able to bless you abundantly, so that in all things at all times, having all that you need, you will abound in every good work.

2 Corinthians 9:8 (NIV)

A GREAT HEALTH DIAGNOSIS from the doctor. The best seat on that long-distance flight. The smile on a child's face after they've blown out all the candles on their birthday cake. Blessings come in all shapes and sizes. What seems like a blessing to one person might not be received as one by another, because we are all so different. But God sees our uniqueness and takes pleasure in the joy He brings as He meets our particular needs.

This special promise God made is quite grand, well beyond our understanding. He is offering us everything we will need today, tomorrow, and forever. At times, it can be difficult for me to keep my own needs in order. How can God possibly keep track of all of ours?

God is all-knowing, and His love knows no bounds. He delights in us as we endeavor to emulate His Son, Jesus. Paul continues in 2 Corinthians 9:10–11 (NIV),

PROMISES TO YOUR LIFE

"Now he who supplies seed to the sower and bread for food will also supply and increase your store of seed and will enlarge the harvest of your righteousness. You will be enriched in every way so that you can be generous on every occasion, and through us your generosity will result in thanksgiving to God."

We can trust that God will take care of us. He provides everything we need to live not just ordinary lives, but to live in abundance. This sense of security gives us the freedom to turn our focus away from ourselves and toward others. We are able to offer those in difficult circumstances help and support when they need it most. The ways we choose to serve others might be as varied as our personalities and gifts. Yet, by showing generosity and abundance with our time, gifts, or funds, we show others to trust that their needs will also be met. In many ways, we become God's hands to a needy world.

God is immeasurably generous, and our generosity might be seen as a reflection of His toward us. The result is a grateful heart for us and for those we serve.

—Heidi Gaul

The King will reply, "What I'm about to tell you is true. Anything you did for one of the least important of these brothers and sisters of mine, you did for me."

Matthew 25:40 (NIRV)

HANDS OF THE FATHER

By Samuel Pennock

FEAR, INSECURITY, AND loneliness are part of my earliest memories. I remember being young and innocent, a loving soul, an honor student, and a good son, but I never really felt normal. By high school, those feelings had progressed into debilitating anxiety, depression, and addiction. When I was exposed to drugs and alcohol I did not even hesitate. I wanted to fit in. I thought I could handle it. Seven years later, I found myself hopeless and unable to stop using. What was at first all fun and games left me broken; a spiritual, emotional, and physical husk; a social deviant; a drug addict; a junkie.

I was nineteen years old and had progressed from just drinking to doing any drug that crossed my path, even using needles to shoot up methamphetamines. Lying, stealing, and disrespecting my parents had become frequent practice. I even physically assaulted my mother, shoving and cursing her if she were in my way. I spent two years in outpatient therapy and twelve-step support groups. I practiced the principles of recovery the best I could. I had hope that what had fixed others could fix me, but sometimes I would sink into despair, overcome by fear, shame, and insecurity. There were times I would be clean and sober for two weeks or a month, but then the blinding compulsion to use drugs and get drunk would hit and I would succumb.

After my last binge, I had promised my therapist and mother that I would sign myself in for long-term in-patient treatment if I used again. That promise came true on April 3, 1983, Easter Sunday, when I found my mother sitting on the front step of our house waiting for me. It was six or seven in the morning. I knew she must have been sitting there all night. That week I checked into an in-patient program.

I was not a model patient. I was continually in trouble for being a smart mouth, for not participating in group, and for bending the rules. To the outside world, I believed, I appeared a crazy and fun-loving guy. I was always terrified that my truth would be exposed—that I was profoundly lonely even in a room full of people. I was crippled with shame, paranoia, anger, and fear. I was teetering on the edge of suicide.

Somehow the little bit of work I'd done and the hundreds of meetings I'd attended planted seeds that would save my life. It came together at an event held in an old converted warehouse called the Bridge.

• • •

The day of the event was a typical day for me—my facade was holding up, and I was quietly watching a young lady I liked in the facility. I was starting to feel better, even though my brokenness and inner secrets still festered in the dark recesses of my mind ready to rush into my consciousness to destroy me. I was feeling a little hopeful.

That night, we were going to watch the movie *The Warriors*, a favorite of mine. But I had bent the rules in some way that day and lost my privileges. I was told to retire to bed. Although I became enraged, I smiled slyly to mask my emotions and headed into the sleeping area. I could smell the pine oil as I entered the large open room, walked through the rows of bunk beds to mine, a top bunk with a view of the high ceiling. My mind raced, mostly cursing the counselors and the place; my stomach churned; I pounded my clenched fists. I let out a guttural *ughhhh* and wanted to scream but would not give them the satisfaction of knowing they got to me.

The inner battle began to rage between staying and leaving. I wanted to walk out but didn't want to deal with this pain any longer. My mind replayed the words I'd been hearing my whole life: "You will never amount to anything." "You are a loser." "Nobody will ever love you." I began to sink into a quicksand of self-pity, despair, and hopelessness. Tears were streaming down my face. It was a short flight of stairs to the roof, then just a step away from escape. I longed for death.

As I thought about taking my own life, I remembered a woman in a meeting who had said suicide was a permanent solution to a temporary problem. And that led to me thinking about the Serenity Prayer: "God, grant me the serenity to accept the things I cannot change, courage to change the things I can, and the wisdom to know the difference."

Then, seemingly out of nowhere, I remembered a character from a recovery meeting nicknamed Jesus Jack. He'd really made an impression on me. He was a full-on biker, with a scruffy beard, chaps, chains, a vest with an eagle patch, and a Harley. He spoke with humility and authority at the same time; he was passionate and funny. He closed with a statement about reaching his end and being on the streets. In a moment of great despair and darkness, he asked God to help him. And God had answered. At that meeting, Jesus Jack said he had not used drugs or alcohol for over ten years. He was free, happy, and full of purpose.

I was in that same place where Jack had been—at my end. I could fight no more. In tears of desperation and rage I cursed God and called out for Him to reveal Himself. Suddenly, two white vaporous hands manifested from above me through the ceiling and slowly cupped and cradled me. As soon as the entity made contact, waves of peace and love washed over and through me. An indescribable sensation of security, safety, and comfort surrounded and engulfed me. My entire body shuddered, goose bumps spread from my head to my feet, and every hair on my body stood straight up.

It was like I was awakening to a new reality. I was becoming a new creation. I was being reborn. I knew intuitively I was in the presence of God; I had called out in desperation and He had reached out to me. I then heard a thundering voice, not audibly but penetrating my heart, spirit, soul, and mind: "You will never drink again, My son."

• • •

A few days later I was ready to leave that program, and a journey of miracles, adventures, tribulations, and great triumphs began. I was a free man full of purpose and hope. Since that otherworldly experience, I have sought God's presence every day. I have found Him in the twelve-step meetings I continue to attend. He speaks through me when I visit prisons and detox centers to share this story of hope, compassion, and love to those still suffering with addiction.

To Jesus Jack and all the others who share their stories, to those who are bold enough to love the unlovable, to people in need, I say: "He sees you! Don't give up hope!"

Prayer for a Hope-Filled Life

Lord, make me an instrument of Your hope and compassion. Give me the courage and the desire to do Your will, shine in Your image, and show Your character to every person I encounter.

Blessed are those who mourn, for they will be comforted.

Matthew 5:4 (NIV)

THE DAY I FOUND HOPE

By Amy Catlin Wozniak

I HAD FAITH AND LOVE but no hope. I'd been searching for it everywhere.

The faith and love I am talking about were pictures hung on our bedroom wall, the words *faith* and *love* written in a scrolling script nestled in ornate brown copper frames.

During the sultry nights that August, I would lie in bed, staring at those pictures while anxious thoughts swirled around in my mind as I tossed and turned, unable to sleep. Closing my eyes would only make things worse. The images I saw there tormented me. Those pictures affixed to the wall reminded me of what I needed to cling to. But it was hard.

Mourning is a roller coaster. Each day, when my eyes would open, my mind would begin searching, trying to find its bearings, and then my memory would awaken to our new reality. I'd close my eyes, cringing from the realization that my stepson, Ryan, was no longer across the hall.

• • •

It had all begun one July evening when Ryan didn't return our texts asking him if he wanted to join us for a dinner of chicken parmesan, one of his favorites. That night, when my husband, Michael, and I went to bed, we left the door unlocked for him as Ryan was prone to leaving his key behind. The following morning, the door was still unlocked. Ryan hadn't come home. We reached out to his friends and family, but no one had heard from him. We all searched for him for two days. On the third day, Michael and I found his body. I can still hear Michael's cries and my scream of "Why, God?" aimed at heaven.

Later, as we sat on the porch of Ryan's stepdad's house, struggling with our shock, the investigators and the coroner pieced together for us what happened. It had been a hot day with little breeze, and Ry had gone to his favorite place in the back acres of his stepdad's farm, as he often did, to hang out. He'd brought a full five-gallon gas can with him to start a bonfire. The day's heat caused a flash point and an explosion that instantly killed Ryan.

Each morning since, the pain, loss, and emptiness would hit me, jockeying for position until I looked at the pictures, calmed by the reminder to focus on my faith and my love of God to survive one day at a time like everyone kept telling me. In my brokenness, I struggled to go on living when Ryan was gone at such a young age.

When I'd purchased those pictures of faith and love, I knew there should be three. The Bible says, "These three remain: faith, hope, and love" (1 Corinthians 13:13, NIV). I would have purchased the picture of hope for my collage wall hanging, but I couldn't find hope in the store. And if you've lost hope...how do you go on from there?

One unseasonably warm late September Saturday, my thirteen-year-old stepdaughter, Madison, was at our house for the weekend. Although I didn't feel like getting out, Maddie needed school supplies, so we decided to take advantage of the nice weather by shopping in the town where Michael and I live. Hartville is a small village planted between the larger cities of Akron and Canton in Ohio, teeming with charming local shops. It also boasts some nationally known locales, like Hartville Hardware, Hartville Kitchen, and the Hartville Chocolate Factory.

Our first stop was the Twice as Nice thrift boutique. My friend Rose, the proprietress, greeted us with "I'm so glad you're here" and gave us a tour of the newly relocated space. We were getting the VIP treatment from Rose, who was helping us find pieces for Maddie's back-to-school wardrobe. By the time we had finished scouring the racks stuffed with fall sweaters, jackets, and jeans, Maddie had scored two fall outfits. We were both smiling as we stowed our packages in the back of our SUV.

"Hi, you guys," my friend Beth called from behind the cash register at the Hartville Chocolate Factory booth at our next stop. We enjoyed looking around at all the handmade chocolates shaped like everything from ballerinas to zoo animals. "Maddie, pick something out. My treat," Beth offered. Maddie's grin spilled over the sides of her chocolate-covered pretzel on our walk to the car. Seeing my friends' smiling faces for the first time in weeks awakened joy inside of me that had been buried in a pit of grief.

We headed to Big Lots on our last stop for back-to-school supplies. As we rolled our cart into the front of the store, a large display of clearance household odds and ends sat in the middle of the aisle. I glanced up, and centered on top was a picture with a flower-printed background in blues, coppers, and golds with a word printed across in big letters.

H–O–P-E.

• • •

"Maddie, there it is," I exclaimed. "I found hope," I said as I snagged the picture from the shelf. It wasn't exactly like my faith and love pictures, but it would match well enough. I carefully placed it in the front of our cart so it didn't get misplaced.

On our way home, I looked over at a smiling Maddie. Seeing her so happy after losing her brother lifted my spirits. We'd had a wonderful day. Suddenly I had an idea. "Let's stop at Aldi on our way home. I want to surprise your dad," I told her.

When Michael got home from work, the first thing he said was, "Hey, it smells good in here." The tangy smell of sausage sautéing with tomatoes filled the room.

"I'm making your favorite." I held out a spoonful of sauce for him to taste. He walked over to the stove. "Lasagna?" He grinned. I'd first made my lasagna recipe for Michael's birthday while we were still dating. Until that day, I hadn't felt like spending time in the kitchen. After the pan was in the oven, he hugged me. "I haven't seen you this happy in a long time." It felt good to be laughing in his arms.

As the three of us sat around the dining room table enjoying the rich, spicy lasagna and garlic bread, Maddie and I shared the story of our day and how it had prompted the special dinner. After we cleaned up the kitchen, we headed upstairs to hang our picture of hope on our bedroom wall, centering it where I could see it from our bed, along with the other two.

The next day, after the closing prayer in church, we met my friend Mindy as we made our way to the church steps. "How are you doing?" she asked as we hugged. Then she said, "Do you think you would be up to trying a few barre classes in Akron with me? I've got a Groupon." She pulled out her phone and showed me the coupon.

My first instinct was to say no, but I stopped myself and gave her my email address so she could forward me the coupon. As we headed for the door, my friend Sherri stopped us and invited me to Amish country with her on Tuesday. This time I said yes without hesitating.

As Michael, Maddie, and I walked down the church steps into the sunshine, the fullness in my heart shone in the fresh tears on my face. Knowing people in the community cared for what we were going through brought tears of joy to my eyes. They didn't insert themselves into our grief but were there for us in subtle, comforting ways.

That night, I recounted our weekend. I knew none of it was a coincidence. Not the meetings with friends, the picture, the will to cook, or the joy I felt. It was as easy to see as the words on those pictures nailed to the wall. God saw my pain and provided what I needed—faith, love, and hope.

I still occasionally wake up in a sweat, haunted by a dream that takes me back to what happened that July day when we found Ryan's body. But these days, when that happens, I look to my left and see Michael. When I see him sleeping peacefully, I am reminded of the strength he's shown since we lost his son. How he's gone on, how we've gone on together and as a family.

And then I glance right, and I see the pictures standing as a reminder that I have faith, hope, and love, everything I need to make it through times of grief and anything else life throws at me because I am rooted in those three things and deeply loved by God.

Prayer for a Hope-Filled Life

Lord, anchor me with faith, hope, and love when I am faced with grief. Help me to focus on You to move forward day by day.

Don't worry about anything; instead, pray about everything. Tell God what you need, and thank him for all he has done.

Philippians 4:6 (NLT)

GOD'S FORMULA FOR HOPE

By Denise Margaret Ackerman

ALTHOUGH IT HAS BEEN more than forty years, I remember the moment as if it happened yesterday. I was seated on the sofa in a friend's brightly decorated living room, my three-month-old daughter cradled in my arms. Barb sat in an armchair across from us as she explained the meaning of a relationship with God. It seemed as if the Lord had turned on a light in my heart and I clearly saw my need to accept Jesus's death on the cross as payment for my sin. I bowed my head and repeated the prayer Barb led: "Lord, please forgive me for my sins. I believe that You died on the cross to pay for my sin, and I invite You to come into my heart."

My faith became personal and alive that day. I felt called to a new purpose: to learn everything I could about the Lord and to share His message with others. God orchestrated a loving support system for me and my family by sending various Christians into my life.

One of my former coworkers introduced me to her cousin Jane. Jane was a new Christian and wanted me to meet her church's pastor. His visit to my home was an eye-opener for me—I never knew that pastors made house calls! Soon after the pastor's visit, Jane asked her friend Kay, who lived nearby, to meet with me. Over the next several months, Kay, a stranger to me, came to my house once a week to teach me the basics of faith and how to study the Bible. These new friends invited my family to attend their church. It was a wonderful experience to learn about God alongside my husband and daughter as we attended Sunday and Wednesday services each week.

• • •

Our little brood expanded, and we were soon a family of five. My husband and I made a big move to an abandoned farm. During the next several years, we homeschooled, remodeled a decrepit farmhouse, raised beef cows, and established a maple syrup business. Life was demanding but good. We had much to be thankful for. Our lives were full as we worked together in our happy corner of God's green earth.

Once our children completed middle school, I felt that homeschooling was not meeting their academic needs, so we took a huge step of faith and enrolled them in a private Christian school fifty miles from our home. The Lord provided a job for me in the vicinity of the campus with hours that coincided with those of the school. I was confident that everything would once again work out. Our oldest child found her niche at the school, but her younger siblings did not.

I prayed for God's direction for their continued education. Since they were not strong academically and were inclined to work with their hands, we thought a vocational school may spark their interest in learning. The following school year, we enrolled the younger two in public school so they could attend the half-day occupational program. God had opened the door for this educational pathway. We were encouraged that everything was going to be better for our teenagers. Things seemed fine—until they weren't.

• • •

Turmoil erupted in our home when our younger two resisted church involvement. They were no longer interested in following the Lord's leading for their lives. I was completely unprepared for this turn of events. Throughout my years attending church and studying God's Word, no one had mentioned that our children might decide to walk away from the faith. I had been steadfast in my example of following the Lord's teaching. I had taught His ways to our children. I had done everything right. Yet our lives were rocked with chaos: fights at school, car accidents, arguments, and even a late-night visit from a police officer.

Desperate to fix the situation, I sought answers. My husband and I met with a Christian counselor in hopes that he would offer suggestions on what steps we could take to redirect our struggling teenagers. Unfortunately, the counselor spent a lot of time talking about himself and digging into my husband's and my childhood experiences. The visits were expensive, and we didn't find the sessions helpful. I read parenting books that focused on teenagers, listened to family-centered radio programs, and sought advice from Christian friends. I cried out to God for guidance on what to do to get our young people back on the right path.

Instead of life getting better, extreme anxiety began to affect my health. I developed insomnia, loss of appetite, and severe headaches. My attempts to control and repair our circumstances had hampered my ability as a wife and mother.

• • •

When I was at my lowest point, I received a phone call from an old friend. She was planning a women's day at her church, and the Lord had prompted her to contact me. Jan invited me to share a devotion centering on the theme planned for this event—hope. It seemed ironic that I was commissioned to speak on a topic that my faith sorely needed. God does work in mysterious ways.

I sought the Lord's help to put together a hope-filled message. I studied the Bible for passages emphasizing the theme. Through the process, God revealed an unexpected remedy for the turmoil I was experiencing in my personal life—changing my focus. Instead of worrying over my offspring's walk away from the faith, I refocused on my own walk of faith. The outline for my speaking event was formed using "hope" as an acrostic.

H—have faith. It was time for me to start living by faith rather than by fear. The Lord reminded me that He is worthy of my trust. His love for my family far exceeds that of my own.

O—open my hands to release my loved ones into the capable hands of the Father. My grip was tight, and the harder I held on, the more anxious I became. Setting my children's spiritual lives free into God's loving hands gave me the freedom from worry that I desperately sought.

P—purpose in my heart to stay the course in my own spiritual walk because that is the only thing that I have control over. God revealed to me that I do not have the power to change someone else's heart—only He can do that. I had made it my goal for my children to live a certain way. A goal is something a person can set for their own life—not for someone else's life. It was time for me to set a new goal—to live a life of hope. With God's help, I redirected my energy to pursue that aspiration.

E—enjoy His blessings amid the angst and heartbreak. It was time for me to take my thoughts captive and choose to be thankful for the good things in my life. I had lost my joy in living because I neglected to give thanks to the Lord.

God reminded me that there were many happy things to focus on. I started journaling God's blessings in my life: knowing Jesus as Savior, my marriage, our lovely home, our free country, and the ways He had provided for our needs. Most importantly, I noted in my journal that God is my source of hope through seasons of testing.

Our three children are now grown and raising teenagers of their own. During my parenting (and grandparenting) years, I have turned to God's formula for hope many times. He's been faithful to me.

Prayer for a Hope-Filled Life

Heavenly Father, I thank You for teaching me how to find hope during the difficult seasons of this life. Please help me to trust You and give thanks while I wait on Your perfect timing. Amen.

Then Peter came to him and asked, "Lord, how often should I forgive someone who sins against me? Seven times?" "No, not seven times," Jesus replied, "but seventy times seven!"

Matthew 18:21–22 (NLT)

FINDING FORGIVENESS, ONE WORD AT A TIME

By Rebecca Hastings

I DIDN'T THINK I COULD ever forgive my father. Maybe the truth was that I didn't want to forgive him. It's hard enough to forgive someone who apologizes and asks for forgiveness. But how do you forgive someone who doesn't even say "I'm sorry" for the pain they caused?

I spent decades living with hurt in my heart. Even as a young girl, I knew my father wasn't present. He chose to leave when I was three. There were interactions and visitations over the years, but when he did show up, he was less dad and more visitor. The older I got, the more I realized he wasn't going to change. I don't even think he was aware of the pain he caused, never mind being sorry.

Over time I learned to live with that pain. I carried it with me everywhere I went like a tiny padlock on my heart, forever connecting me to the pain. It felt like my pain would be locked there forever, another symbol of the hurt he caused. I felt helpless to change it.

As a believer, I knew what God said regarding forgiveness. He offered it freely to me, and I was supposed to do the same to others. But did that really apply if the person wasn't sorry?

One day I came across the verses in Matthew when Peter asked Jesus how many times he should forgive someone who sins against him. Jesus's reply was simple yet bold: 70 times 7 times. That's 490 times.

Jesus told Peter to forgive someone 490 times, and I hadn't even forgiven my father once. Some translations give a number lower than 77, but the message is still the same. Jesus calls us to forgive so many times it seems ridiculous. It feels unjust.

I was called to be obedient to Jesus. The idea of forgiving my father felt impossible, but I wondered what I had to lose. At worst, forgiving my father was undeserved and a waste of my time. At best? I didn't even know.

Could God's promises of hope and freedom that come when we walk in His ways really apply here, when my father and I didn't even speak? Would God really be faithful to help me with this?

I decided to go for it. I didn't want to skirt my responsibility, so I went with the bigger number. I decided I would forgive my father 490 times a day until it didn't hurt so much. Maybe if I forgave my father the way Jesus called me to, that padlock on my heart would unlock and I would be free. I didn't have an end date, I simply needed to walk in obedience and see what God would do. The idea felt risky. But hope often does.

• • •

I was overwhelmed before I even started. But saying the words "I forgive him" 490 times doesn't take as long as one would think. At a regular pace, I calculated it would take about eight minutes to say "I forgive him" out loud almost 500 times. This was about half of my ride to work every day, the perfect time for me to be alone and give this experiment a try. I would start each day when I left my house and forgive my father for eight minutes as I drove.

The first day, I started my Honda Accord without turning on the radio like I usually did. As I backed out of my driveway and made my way down the windy road, I said out loud: "I forgive him. I forgive him. I forgive him. I forgive..."

The words felt empty on my tongue. But I continued. I heard myself saying them, the phrase sounding rote, the way you recite state capitals or math facts you don't really care about. They were simply words, repeated again and again for eight minutes.

When I made it to the stopping place, my jaw hurt and I didn't want to say another word so I drove the rest of the way in silence. Surely tomorrow would be better.

But it wasn't. Neither was the next day. This empty recitation lasted for weeks. Weeks of me simply showing up, wondering if God was really there. Wondering if this even mattered. Wondering if I was crazy. Could I really forgive my father even if he didn't ask for it? I wondered so many things. But still, I kept going. Something inside me knew I needed to.

As I continued, tiny changes began to happen. One day I noticed that my jaw wasn't as tight. A bit later I found myself slowing down, really listening to the words I was saying and allowing them to sink into my soul as a combination of question and declaration of faith. Sometimes the words felt like an exhale, something releasing from within me with every recitation. Each of these little changes made space for something new in my heart: hope.

Maybe I could really forgive my father.

As I kept going, I felt some momentum build. I began looking forward to those minutes in my car each morning. I wasn't sure what forgiveness felt like, but I could feel that things were different. Something in me felt different. And then I noticed something new.

I'm not sure what day it was, but I noticed that it didn't hurt to say the words. When my father came to mind, I wasn't tied up in grief or anger. I could think about him without the baggage of the previous years of pain. It was as if that old, rusted padlock on my heart had finally been loosened.

• • •

I kept going. Weeks turned to months. I didn't forgive my father merely with a passing statement. I was finding forgiveness each time I spoke the words "I forgive you." Time didn't heal my wounds. Forgiveness healed my wounds. God met me in my car each day, each time I uttered that simple phrase. He met me in that place, faithful to His promises to help me and be with me always.

Forgiveness wasn't something I did. Forgiveness was something I found, one word at a time, stacked in eight-minute blocks. It was extravagant and tedious, undeserved and required, messy and beautiful. It was the key that freed me in a way I never thought—or hoped—possible.

Today, when I think about my father I am no longer bound by anger or pain. Nothing has changed between us, but everything has changed within me. And when I feel uncertain, God reminds me that there is freedom in forgiveness, even if it takes 490 tries.

Prayer for a Hope-Filled Life

Lord, I want to walk in obedience and forgive fully. Walk with me and help me learn to offer extravagant forgiveness, that I may find freedom and hope in You. Amen.

I give them eternal life, and they shall never perish; no one will snatch them out of my hand. My Father, who has given them to me, is greater than all; no one can snatch them out of my Father's hand.

John 10:28–29 (NIV)

FOR MANY OF US, the struggle to do the right thing can seem both exhausting and daunting. We mess up or make a bad decision, much as we try to avoid it. Afterward, we might be left wondering where we stand with God. Could Satan snatch us away, never to be restored to our place as part of God's family? Could our sins, no matter how small, be our everlasting undoing?

The short answer is no, and we learn this from these verses in John 10. This passage gives us hope in concentrated form. The person we can trust more than anyone else is promising us we will live forever in His presence. No one—and nothing—can separate us from Him. This is divine grace at its fullest. Could anything be more hope-filled?

PROMISES TO YOUR LIFE

At the end of verse 29, Jesus reiterates that we can't be snatched away, because God won't allow it to happen. This passage makes me think that Jesus knows some of us might still be uncertain about our future and therefore need an extended double eternal warranty on top of His Word. He knows us well. If you're like me, you might understand how trust can be a real challenge. I want—and need—a promise, something I can depend on. Like the father asking Jesus to heal his son in Mark 9:24 (NIV), I say, "I do believe; help me overcome my unbelief."

But this isn't a costly insurance policy purchased to cover breakage on an appliance or car. Instead, this promise cost us nothing, though it cost Jesus everything. This promise cannot and will not ever be broken. It's in writing in the pages of the Bible, and like all of God's promises, it stands firm and invulnerable. We can count on it to be true. Like all of God's promises, it will come to pass and is already happening in our daily lives.

We are safe. We are blessed. We are chosen. We can walk with pride and confidence, secure in the knowledge that our future is bright. Guaranteed.

—Heidi Gaul

For we are God's handiwork, created in Christ Jesus to do good works, which God prepared in advance for us to do.

Ephesians 2:10 (NIV)

A WORK IN PROGRESS

By Jennifer Hutmire

HER BIG BLUE EYES filled with tears as she poured out her heart to me. I prayed with the woman sitting across from me and let her know that even though her life seemed hopeless at the moment, I would hold onto hope for her until she was able to do so for herself. She squeezed my hand, grateful to be seen and heard in a way only possible by someone else who was well acquainted with pain. In that moment, I thanked God for the circumstances in my life that enabled me to comfort this woman in her time of need. I was grateful for the way God had redeemed my suffering by using it to help me serve Him with compassion and grace.

• • •

I hadn't always held this perspective. I had been dealing with chronic illness for many years. In the past, I wasn't able to see beyond the pain of the present moment. I remember sitting hunched over on my bed in the dark, deeply discouraged and unsure about how I could possibly carry on. I was not surprised to discover that the suicide rate for those with chronic illness is very high. It's hard to face a future in which pain, fatigue, and other symptoms will continue endlessly with no cure in sight. After years of struggling with unrelenting physical pain from multiple chronic health issues, as well as emotional pain from childhood traumas, I contemplated giving up on life.

Coping with the symptoms of my health problems wasn't even the worst part. The most difficult thing to deal with was the huge gap between the life I'd always envisioned and the reality of my current circumstances. I had planned on becoming a full-time missionary ever since my family served as missionaries in Mexico when I was a child, but I was disqualified due to my health problems. I'd also dreamed of traveling the world as a professional speaker, encouraging large groups of women at conferences and retreats. How could I do that when I could barely make it to the bathroom and back to my bed without assistance?

I had always imagined myself as a wonderful mother and homemaker—baking bread, sewing my own curtains, and providing my children with educational activities. I pictured us enjoying excursions to the library, zoo, and museums.

Instead, I was a mess, my house was a wreck, we were living in poverty due to my inability to work, and my children were in the other room huddled in front of the TV.

In my mind, clouded as it was with the hopelessness that comes from depression, giving up on this life wouldn't be a selfish act because I honestly believed everyone would be better off without me. I thought that if I was gone, I would set those around me free from the burden of having to take care of me.

I had always been the strong one, the person others had gone to for help, but now I could barely take care of myself. I even felt like I had disappointed God, and I worried that He would regret saving me and adopting me into His family. It felt like all of my dreams for serving the Lord had shriveled up in the reality of my discouraging circumstances.

• • •

Miraculously, that day, that moment when the darkness seemed to be closing in, God shone the light of His love into my troubled mind when my husband entered the room. Having walked beside me along this painful road for years, he understood the difficulty I was having and the reasons I wanted to end my life. However, he reminded me that God was not done with me yet. He said, "Jen, if you give up now, you will never have the chance to witness the ways that He will be working in and through you to make a difference for His Kingdom."

Those words hit me like a thunderbolt. My husband was right. I had to trust that God created me for a purpose. Even if I didn't understand what that purpose was, I could trust that He was still at work within me and that my life had meaning. Knowing that the Creator was shaping my life into His masterpiece provided the hope I needed.

Since then, I have seen God use me to make a positive difference in the lives of others, not only despite my pain, but *because* of it. I am able to recognize people who are hurting even when they try to cover up their pain. I can listen to them, pray for them, and offer encouragement based on my own experiences. I may not be the supermom I'd dreamed of becoming, but my three sons grew up to be compassionate, resourceful young men who knew they were dearly loved. They also learned to be grateful for what they had in the midst of a self-centered, materialistic society.

• • •

Even though I am not a career missionary, I am allowing God's love to flow through me and into the lives of others. I was wrong to think He is disappointed in me for not accomplishing more for Him because He created me and equipped me to do the specific work He prepared for me to do, knowing in advance the struggles I would have. I have faith that my suffering serves a purpose—His purpose. Just as He showed the Apostle Paul, God has helped me to see that His strength is made perfect in my weakness. Because of my challenges, any success that I have is clearly due to God's power at work within me.

Though I still experience daily pain and fatigue, new medications and procedures have made a positive difference in my health. New technology has opened up opportunities to reach out even when I am unable to leave the house. I never thought I could volunteer at church because my health issues are very unpredictable. But now I can connect through Zoom or FaceTime.

After experiencing the life-changing power of hope, I am now teaching a women's Sunday school class in which I am encouraging others to hold onto hope in the midst of their own suffering. If I'm unable to teach due to my health, someone else can teach it for me using the study guide I created.

Rather than focusing on what I can't do, I choose to remember that God has prepared good works that He specifically equipped me to do. My circumstances might continue to tempt me to give up, but I will not allow them to prevent me from serving God. Holding onto this hope is not a one-time event but rather an act of faith I must make over and over as God continues to work in and through me.

Prayer for a Hope-Filled Life

Lord, help me to remember that You have a purpose for me. When circumstances make me feel like giving up hope, I can trust that You will make something beautiful from the broken pieces of my life.

Let the peace of Christ rule in your hearts, since as members of one body you were called to peace. And be thankful.

Colossians 3:15 (NIV)

A HEART FULL OF GOD

By Kathie Kania

"IT'S A TYPE OF HEART failure," my cardiologist explained to my husband, Michael, and me as the nurses wheeled away the heart catheterization equipment. I was groggy from the anesthetic, blinking and looking fearful, and the doctor turned to me: "It's not *exactly* like the kind your mother had, but similar."

"She lived to be almost ninety-six," I smiled tremulously.

"Good incentive," he agreed. "We'll get you on some good meds. But I want you to take it easy for a week—no pressure on that incision. No lifting. Then we'll talk about diet and exercise to help you."

"I can manage this," I told a concerned Michael in the car. "Think of how active Mom was in her retirement years. I'll do my best to get past this fatigue and live normally, just as she did."

Over the next week I studied the papers the doctor gave me, including the illustrated pamphlet that showed carefree people going about their business in spite of heart failure. I studied heart failure online. I bought a "heart diet" cookbook.

But I knew I had even *better*, more personal information, tailored to my particular gene pool. I went right to my bookshelf that held those old diaries: mine and my mother's. Then I settled in with a much-handled little book—her 1986 diary, the year Mom was diagnosed.

"I hope her journal will help me get the edge on this condition," I said to my husband. "I'm going to find Mom's symptoms. I'm going to see how she felt and what meds she took. I'm going to see just what she *did*. Since it's hereditary, I'm going to gather all the heart info I can from Mom."

I couldn't think of a time when Mom had not been optimistic and active, and though her heart failure slowed her for a while, it seemed she was soon right back to helping neighbors get their groceries, teaching Sunday school, haunting Kmart for blue light specials.

• • •

My darling mother had left us in January 2015, slipping quietly home to the Savior she adored. How I had missed her kindly assurance of prayer over the phone and her sympathetic ear as I dealt with my increasing symptoms of fatigue and what we (and even my general practitioner) had thought was asthma. I guessed her diaries were the next best thing to her being there. I was sure she'd have listed each discomfort and worry in her journal as I'd done in mine. I would nod and gain insight as I read.

"Here it is," I called to Michael. In her tiny cursive, she had written, "I walked down to the mailbox this morning and had to stop and rest before I got back to the house. I was so out of breath. Maybe I'll ask Dr. Kitchen about this."

"OK," I muttered. "Let's see what tests she had." I flipped a few pages.

"They did some testing," Mom wrote. Hmm. Mom didn't seem very worried, like I had been when I had written a dissertation of my heart catheterization and sonogram with the clarity of a textbook in my diary. But then, wasn't she *always* leaving things with the Lord? This was serious, though; this was heart failure.

Well, it would be interesting to see what medicines they put her on. I had studied mine online, scrutinizing every single side effect. Watching for dizziness. Waiting for any nausea. Taking the meds on time, with military precision.

Mom had this to say: "I have to take K-Dur and Imdur, and I laugh every time I say those two funny names." I rolled my eyes. I read further, looking for any helpful heart information that Mom might have made mention of, but found nothing except an occasional doctor visit for a checkup, where she was "doing fine." "I'm so thankful," she'd added.

There was no more mention of fatigue or complaints about meds, discomfort, or worry.

Instead, Mom wrote of people: "Kimbles brought us the nicest banana bread this evening! I was so grateful!" "I drove Ann to get groceries, and she bought our lunch—what a blessing!" My diary spoke of people too, but more often than not, I went on a rant about some know-it-all at work or church.

Mom set "memory scenes": "Bud and I took sandwiches to Freeport Beach and watched the sunset tonight. Beautiful." "Mooneys and Pratts came, and we all made cider in our press. Twelve gallons!" These were things I recalled, too, and it was fun to relive them.

Mom wrote one-sentence synopses of Sunday sermons: "Pastor Don said that when we worship, it's actually God who is in the audience, not us." Wow.

No more entries about her heart or how she was feeling until I stumbled upon one from the day Mom needed a reasonable favor from someone close to her. This person not only refused but became angry and indignant. "I really wish this had gone differently," Mom had written. Amazingly, Mom continued to write of get-togethers that included this person, even after this happened. I did discover that, months later, the person relented, and Mom got her wish. But not a negative word was written about the woman. Only "Praise the Lord!" when the situation turned.

I knew full well that my journal would've blazed with fiery verbal volcanics had the same thing happened to me!

But not Mom's. Her entries reflected a calm, faith-filled life of knowing that "all things work together for good to those who love God, to those who are the called according to His purpose" (Romans 8:28, NKJV). She didn't just know this, she *lived* this. Her assurance smoothed her day-to-day life despite anything that came her way, from angry resistance to heart disease. In real life we had seen her serene faith, and it was reflected, of course, in her diary.

• • •

Was my diary like Mom's at all? I flipped through one. No. Events and prayers, to be sure, but stream-of-consciousness worry, health complaints, righteous (and not-so-righteous) indignation over slights.

When I'm gone, do I want anyone to read my journal? Will the reader feel assured? Will she gain any insight, comfort, or help? Any info on what to do to have a healthy heart? A heart that is full and overflowing with thanks to God?

I was hopeful I would discover the secret to Mom's long life in her diary. Those pages didn't give me the heart info I was looking for—they gave me much better heart info! I know that my journal will begin to read differently from now on.

Prayer for a Hope-Filled Life

Dear Lord, teach me to look beyond my own worries and difficulties and to put my trust in Your constant care and love.

Though the mountains be shaken and the hills be removed, yet my unfailing love for you will not be shaken nor my covenant of peace be removed.

Isaiah 54:10 (NIV)

THE ANNIVERSARY TRIP

By Amanda Pennock

IT WAS A BEAUTIFUL crisp fall morning as I headed to the Virginia mountains to celebrate my thirty-ninth wedding anniversary. My husband and I had made this trip almost every year together. This time, however, I was alone. My husband was filing for divorce, other areas of my life were falling apart, and I even had thoughts of suicide. I had lost all hope and could not find any peace in my heart or mind. I felt that I had lost all control of my life.

Even through this heartache, I knew God wanted me to know that He had me, that He was in control. I just had to be willing to let Him take control of my life. I felt I really needed to make this trip. I would be experiencing the same places my husband and I had over the years, but this time it would be just God and me. My friends and family were very concerned for me and didn't think I should go, but I knew God had something special in store for me.

As I drove the four-hour trip, I passed by all our favorite wineries. No wineries for me this time, though. I had been sober for just over three months after having reached my bottom and admitted I was powerless where alcohol was concerned. I also noticed that the scenery looked different this time, perhaps because I was able to notice God's beauty everywhere. All through the rolling hills, frost covered the grass and the rooftops. I saw the vivid fall colors throughout the trees. I remember in the past being so disappointed if there wasn't a lot of color. This time, however, all I felt was gratitude and peace. It was as if blinders had been removed from my eyes and I could see everything clearly.

• • •

When I arrived in the mountains, I felt God's presence everywhere. I had stopped and picked up some chicken for a picnic. I found the perfect spot by a fallen tree branch, in a place called Big Meadows. My husband and I had stopped here many times; we'd even stayed at the inn and the campground. I put out my blanket and started eating lunch. After finishing the picnic, I decided to drive down Skyline Drive through the Shenandoah National Park and get in some hiking. I found a place to park and hiked out to the ridge. When I reached the edge, the view took my breath away. "Oh God, thank You so much for sharing Your beauty with me," I whispered. I found a large rock to sit on and take everything in. It was a windy day—it was as if God was blowing His breath on me.

After resting in His presence at the ridge, it was time to head to my hotel. I was at the same resort my husband and I'd stayed in many times. I checked in and went to my room to unpack and settle in. It had been a long, emotional day. My room had a balcony, so I opened the door and headed out. There were trees surrounding me. I felt as if I was in a tree house. I sat down in the chair and was taking in all the visual beauty when I noticed the sounds. The wind blowing through the trees sounded like clapping hands. I remembered reading a Bible scripture about trees clapping. I was so filled with excitement that I ran back into the room and opened my Bible.

I couldn't believe my eyes when I started reading Isaiah 55:12 (NIV): "You will go out in joy and be led forth in peace; the mountains and hills will burst into song before you, and all the trees of the field will clap their hands." I felt consumed with His presence. The God of the universe was right there in the hotel room with me. It was as if time stood still as I was filled with peace. As I continued to read, I was directed to another passage across the page of the Bible in Isaiah. In Isaiah 54:4–6 (NIV), I read, "'You will forget the shame of your youth and remember no more the reproach of your widowhood. For your Maker is your husband—the Lord Almighty is His name—the Holy One of Israel is your Redeemer; he is called the God of all the earth. The LORD will call you back as if you were a wife deserted and distressed in spirit—a wife who married young only to rejected,' says your God."

Wow! God was speaking directly to me through His Word. He was letting me know that He would be my husband, my provider, my everything. At that very moment, I knew that no matter what happened, everything was going to be all right. He had given me the hope that I needed to keep going. I needed only to trust in Him and take one day at a time.

• • •

The next morning, I woke up a new person. I felt that I had been given another chance in life, a brand-new beginning. However, instead of me trying to be in control of my life, this time I would let my new husband and provider (God) take control.

When I arrived back home after that life-changing trip, I had a purpose and a reason for living. I got involved in volunteering at a recovery center to help others find hope and peace. I became more involved in church and started singing in the choir. I designated Friday evenings as date night with God, my new husband. I would go down to a wildlife sanctuary, look out over the bay, and talk with my love.

This trip was seven years ago. Since then, I met a wonderful, strong Christian man and remarried. I never thought that I would love again, but God had a plan. My new husband and I are retired and travel all around the country. God has given me the ability to start making jewelry, and I write encouraging scriptures on little note cards and place them with each piece of jewelry. As we travel, I leave behind a piece of handmade jewelry and note as a way to give back what was given me—hope!

On that anniversary trip, I had gone to the mountains a broken person filled with pain and no hope of a future. But because of my travel companion—God—I came back with a brand-new life filled with hope, purpose, peace, and a love like I have never known.

Prayer for a Hope-Filled Life

Oh Father, I give myself to You each day. On days when I feel lost, remind me of Your great promises. You are with me and will never leave me. You know what tomorrow brings and I do not. Help me to be willing to put my trust in You, living one day at a time and remembering that Your mercies are new every morning. Amen.

I will lead the blind by ways they have not known, along unfamiliar paths I will guide them; I will turn the darkness into light before them and make the rough places smooth.

Isaiah 42:16 (NIV)

OUR DIVINE TRAVEL GUIDE

By Claire McGarry

WHEN COVID HIT, my kids were fifteen, thirteen, and nine. Trying to emphasize the positive, I viewed quarantine as my opportunity to draw my kids back in and away from the outside influences that were pulling them away from Christ. Toward that end, I'd gather them together every day in prayer after remote learning, re-rooting them in the One who would see us through. After, we'd play a game together for quality fun. It was a great routine, one that was working. It provided them with structure in a crazy time, protected them from the fear that permeated the world, and gave them something to look forward to each day.

But even a good routine can grow stale over time, especially when you're a teenager and you're cooped up. Consequently, my boys' grades began to plummet. When you're fifteen and thirteen, computers are for gaming, not learning. It turns out that it was easier, and far more fun, for Zack and Mason to click over to video games on their laptops than it was to participate in class. No matter how hard the teachers worked to make the content interesting and engaging, they just couldn't compete with that. How I longed for old-fashioned textbooks and pen on paper so my kids wouldn't have the gaming temptation right at their fingertips on the very devices they were supposed to be learning on.

For her part, Jocelyn was doing her best to stay focused. But at nine years of age, she just wasn't grasping some of the math concepts taught via Zoom. She's a responsible and conscientious little girl. Not being able to conquer the material was taking its toll on her. As bad grade after bad grade rolled in, I tried every parenting trick in the book to get each of them back on track. With every tactic that didn't work, they got more irritated and I got more frustrated. We were all just hanging on to the hope that in-person school would resume soon.

The day our governor announced that remote learning would continue through to the end of the school year was a bad day in our home. None of us wanted to accept that this new form of learning, that didn't work for any of my kids, was going to be their reality for the duration. It was only April. That meant two more months of torture. Eight weeks is a *very* long time in the lives of kids, especially when the majority of those eight weeks would be spent on something they were literally failing at. Worse yet, school vacation week, the reprieve we'd all been waiting for, had been whittled down to just two days. Our school district decided it would be better to shorten our time off so we'd meet the required 180 days sooner and end the academic year early.

I knew it fell to me to somehow make the most of that short break to turn around the mood in my home. But how? We couldn't go anywhere. Sure, my kids wouldn't have to Zoom into their classes, but we'd still be stuck within the same four walls we'd been restricted to for weeks. Typically, I'm extremely resourceful and very creative. But with this conundrum in front of me, and my creative side depleted, I knew for certain Jesus was the only answer.

• • •

I turned to Him that Saturday in my prayer time. Although He already knew every detail of our situation, I still poured it all out at His feet. It was the only way to completely empty myself so there'd be room for Him to refill me. And refill me He did! As the floodgate of ideas opened, I couldn't write fast enough to capture them all in my journal. Once I did, I got to work in partnering with Him to bring it all to life.

On the first morning of school vacation, I ran around with excitement, announcing that we were going on a trip. I asked my kids and husband to take the suitcases I'd packed out the front door and into the car. They were completely befuddled. But my enthusiasm had them racing outside. I jumped behind the wheel of our minivan and pulled out of the driveway as they bombarded me with: "Where are we going?" "I thought the world was shut down." "I thought we weren't allowed to travel." I just smiled and told them they'd have to wait and see.

They didn't think it was unusual when I took them through the drive-through of our local doughnut shop. But rather than getting doughnuts, I ordered bagels instead. When I drove back home, their confusion escalated. Nonetheless, I walked them up the basement steps, pointed to the sign I'd taped to the basement door earlier that morning, and read it aloud exclaiming, "Welcome to your World Tour!" I then led them to the TV, where I'd preloaded a travel video on Israel.

As we sat munching our bagels, our four walls melted away as we were transported to the continent of Asia and the beautiful streets inside the holy walls of Jerusalem. When the video ended, I placed shish kebab skewers on the kitchen floor and explained the rules of "Three Sticks," a traditional schoolyard game the children of Israel play. My kids were all about jumping between the skewers, extending them farther and farther apart to see who could jump the farthest without stepping more than once between the sticks.

By then, it was lunchtime. Back we went into the car and through another drive-through. When we came home, it was to the continent of North America. While eating McDonald's food, picnic-style on the family room rug, this travel video took us to Washington, D.C., where we explored all the beautiful monuments commemorating the incredible people and events that shaped our country. When it was over, we cleared out space in the dining room and kitchen so we could divide into teams and play the game Massachusetts' YMCA physical director, William Morgan, invented in 1895. Using a piece of streamer taped to the doorway between the two rooms, I created a volleyball court and produced the balloon we'd use as our ball. At this point, my kids were ready to move. They put everything they had into getting the balloon over that makeshift net!

Burning every calorie we'd had at lunch, we were more than ready for our afternoon snack of chips and salsa as we moved on to South America and the travel video that showed us the wonders of the ancient ruins of Machu Picchu in Peru. That was followed by the Peruvian classroom game of "El conejo es muy vivo y el lobo es muy tonto" (The rabbit is very lively and the wolf is very foolish). As the five of us sat in a circle with a blanket over our laps, the person who was the "lobo" (wolf) sat in the middle trying to catch the "conejo" (rabbit, a.k.a. stuffed animal) that we passed around under the blanket.

After sitting for so long, it was the ideal time to go for a passeggiata (evening stroll), perfectly aligning with what the Italians do as our tour moved on to the continent of Europe. We got back from our walk to find the pizza I'd secretly ordered before we left waiting for us on our doorstep. We devoured that as the next travel video took us around the countryside of Italy. Our competitive streak revved up again for "Corsa con la cannata" (pitcher races) in the backyard. With pitchers of water balanced on our heads, we raced to see who could walk the fastest from one orange cone to another without spilling a drop.

The long and exciting day wound down as we explored the continent of Africa. Many regions of Africa are known for their spicy ice cream, so we made our own ice cream sundaes before going on safari in Tanzania. That sugared us up for the lively game of "Mbube, Mbube" (lion, lion). Blindfolding one person as the lion and another as the impala, we spun them both and helped the lion capture the impala by chanting "mbube, mbube" louder and softer depending on how close or far away the lion was.

Looking back on that magical day, I can see the hand of Jesus at every turn. We were on an unfamiliar path, in dark circumstances. Yet like always, He made the rough places smooth by providing what we needed. He gave me every single idea for that virtual world tour, as well as the wherewithal to pull it all off. He gave my family the open minds and hearts to participate with joy and enthusiasm. As a result, we were rejuvenated and renewed enough to make it through until summer.

Prayer for a Hope-Filled Life

Gracious Guide, prompt us to turn to You in the midst of our darkness so You can shine Your light into the difficult circumstances of our days. Amen.

Once I was young, and now I am old. Yet I have never seen the godly abandoned or their children begging for bread.

Psalm 37:25 (NLT)

PROVISION AWAITS ON THE OTHER SIDE

By Kenneth Avon White

WHEN I DECIDED TO uproot my life from the people and places I'd known for the past twenty years, it was mostly in response to a need for solace. The aftershocks of 9/11 continued to have ripple effects. From my perch it felt like the wheels of commerce in Washington, DC, had come to a grinding halt. It wasn't long after that dark day when I was downsized from my job in public relations because business had evaporated. Promoting special causes and initiatives took a back seat to finding those responsible for the terror attacks. On top of all this, my closest friend and landlord suffered a stroke. This was devasting in itself but I lost my housing in the process. Yet the underlying force driving me to flee was my growing angst about living in a "target" city.

Much like the *Mayflower*'s Pilgrims, passengers on the Underground Railroad, and Europe's poor who set their sights on Lady Liberty, I took a leap of faith. I imagine the entire collective must have been of the same mindset as I declared to myself, *There must be something better out there, and with God's help, I'm going to find it.*

My somewhere was Tennessee, where my sister lived. I found a room for rent in a home in Nashville to preserve my meager savings. I shipped several boxes of belongings, gave away what didn't fit in a box, threw the rest of my things in the trunk of my car, and hit the road.

• • •

Nashville appealed to me because it's a city of dreamers like me. My dream was a bit different from most. I wanted to land my dream job in public relations within Christian music or book publishing. The dreamers I knew were singers in search of a record deal or book authors looking to have their first book published. The only thing bigger in Nashville than country music is Christian music, with Christian book publishing not far behind.

Unfortunately, my first two years in Music City was one big sour note. Every résumé I sent out hit a brick wall. I eventually caught on that there were no large public relations firms like there were in Washington and what work there was got farmed out to freelancers.

To make ends meet, I turned to waiting tables at a restaurant not far from Nashville's Music Row, a place many record labels and music studios call home. The transition from desk job to carting around heavy trays of food was grueling. The irony of it all was not lost on me. I went from dining with Washington influencers to serving dinner to Nashville's music industry insiders.

I didn't pray about my move. I didn't even casually ask God for guidance. But by His grace and love I was led to an oasis in the desert of Nashville called Belmont Church. The worship was unlike anything I had experienced and ushered me right into the throne room of heaven. The preaching brought me deeper into Scripture than I'd ever been. My small group provided me with much-needed support. And the focus on prayer taught me to pray and be prayed for in ways I'd never done before.

Despite not consulting God about the huge life decision I'd made, I knew His promise of provision was not hemmed in by my lack of wisdom. So I kept putting out résumés for jobs that even remotely resembled my dream job. Until it happened, I knew God would provide for my needs based on how He'd come through so many times before.

I did find hope that better days were ahead when God provided me a way out of waiting tables. The work was sporadic and ran the gamut from stuffing envelopes to running payroll timeclock cards through scanning machines. This job required me to take a bus to the end of the line and then walk another quarter mile along the road to get to the work site. But I was grateful and continued to keep my antenna held high to make sure I heard God clearly on my next steps to that better place. Then, I unexpectedly picked up His signal one prayer night at church.

The evening was full of anticipation. These periodic nights of worship and prayer ministry by trained prayer warriors were known for ushering in breakthroughs in the spiritual and natural realms. Not long into my ministry time, my prayer warrior looked me straight in the eyes and said, "I feel God wants me to tell you to cast your net on the other side of the boat." She prayed words about looking in the wrong place and the frustration attached and the challenges of just getting by. She ended by clutching my hands firmly, staring me down, and stressing the importance of "casting my net on the other side of the boat." Her words made sense to me even though I'm not sure they did to her.

I was familiar with the scriptures that tell of the miracle Jesus performed when Peter and the other apostles returned to shore after a long day of fishing with nothing to show for it. At Jesus's instruction, and with great reluctance because he knew better, Peter cast his net on the other side of the boat from where they'd been looking. Up from the waters came a net bursting at the seams with fish—a haul that would feed their families with a bounty left over to sell.

But this night I discovered something new. This story was just as much about God's promise of provision as it was about Jesus the performer of miracles. On this night it became clear that like Peter, I had to let go of what I knew in order to get to God's place of provision. I knew I had to expand my thinking on where to look for work and what type of work to look for.

The next day, I began to cast my résumé on the other side of where I'd thought my catch would come. I registered with employment agencies specializing in more mainstream industries. It wasn't long before I parlayed my public relations writing skills into a technical writer position. One year later I was promoted to communications and change readiness manager based on my communications degree.

Unfortunately, that job came to an end with the financial crisis of 2008. Though that road ended, the path God had set me on did not. I went on to hold positions as a technical writer and business analyst that saw my pay increase substantially with each new employer.

This increase in salary helped me pay the six thousand dollars to receive certification as an organizational change manager, a practitioner who helps employees adjust to change. After certification, it took just two short contract positions before I landed a full-time job as a change management specialist blessed with enough money that I was able to save for the down payment on my first house and buy a car.

But even with this overflow, I didn't have enough to make up for lost time saving for retirement. My plans were to work longer, scale my lifestyle down, and save big to reach the scant retirement savings goal I thought possible. But then God showed up in disguise.

• • •

Losing my job again didn't seem like part of a miracle in the making, but it was. I was on the brink of becoming downsized for the third time, and doubts crept in about where my career was going and the ability to save for retirement. Then, with four weeks left of employment and at the beginning of the COVID-19 pandemic, when companies began to pull back, God miraculously promoted me into management with a highly regarded company and a pay increase. I say miraculously because what are the odds that on a five-thousand-person work campus, the person sitting next to the hiring manager was best friends with my current supervisor, who told her friend they'd be crazy if they didn't hire me?

In three short years, with four more years to work, I have already saved triple that scant amount of money I thought I'd be able to cobble together for retirement. The most surreal part of it all is that I'm now in need of a financial adviser. God is good. All the time. Yes, and amen.

I know now that God my heavenly Father finds pleasure in providing for this child of His. Even when I don't apply wisdom to my decisions, outright avoid God's counsel, or let doubts fester, He is forevermore faithful. In this I find hope, rest, and solace.

Prayer for a Hope-Filled Life

Father, help me clearly hear Your instructions so that I can follow Your plan of sustained provision for my life.

He has made everything beautiful in its time. He has also set eternity in the human heart; yet no one can fathom what God has done from beginning to end.

Ecclesiastes 3:11 (NIV)

BEAUTIFUL IN ITS TIME

By Adria Wilkins

I NEVER THOUGHT MUCH about emergency medical helicopters until we needed one.

We were living in Paris, Texas, when our son Blake was born with spina bifida. He needed to be flown by helicopter to Dallas for emergency back surgery. I was able to see my son for just a few minutes after his birth before the medical team whisked him away. I had to place my newborn in the hands of people I didn't know in a helicopter owned by CareFlite. I was scared, yet felt peace after meeting the medical staff. They assured me they would give him the utmost care.

"Making Precious Minutes Count" has been CareFlite's motto for more than forty years. Their mission is to bring help and hope to all who need medical transport. I didn't know it then, but this motto of hope would become mine too.

Our home was two hours away, so we rented a hotel room about a mile from the hospital. My husband and I took turns staying in Dallas while the other went home to be with our five-year-old daughter.

My sister came in from Nashville to be with me for a couple of days. One morning I woke up with a song in my head called "In His Time," based on Ecclesiastes 3:11. The song and scripture brought hope to my soul and brought with it a knowing, a feeling of peace that "He has made everything beautiful its time" (NIV).

• • •

Beauty comes in many forms and in ways we least expect it. What is beautiful to some people may be beautiful in a different way for others. I decided to claim this promise in Ecclesiastes and carry it with me through our long road ahead.

I journaled my thoughts and prayers from the very beginning of our son's life in a journal inscribed with the words of Ecclesiastes 3:11. These were reminders each day of the hope God had placed in my heart with this song and scripture.

My husband set up a website for people to see pictures and get updates on Blake. Even though he didn't get out of the house much because of his acute medical care, Blake touched many people's lives. Some told us he encouraged them and made them smile. Others said, "If Blake can go through all the medical stuff he does, then I can get through my medical stuff." One man even told us that Blake's life saved his marriage.

We arrived safely at home, and for the first time in three months, we were all together under one roof. We had twenty-four-hour home health care and our home became a busy place with people in and out. Every day was a celebration to be home as a family, and our goal was to make life as normal as possible for our family even with Blake's medical condition.

The days were long and hard as we cared for our son, yet we held on to every precious minute with Blake. As the days turned into months and years, I leaned in a little closer to the verse that reminds us that God makes everything beautiful in its time.

Little Blake was on a ventilator all his life, but he didn't let that stop him. He was always smiling and blowing kisses. He learned to sign fifteen words. He played and made a mess just like all toddlers.

Blake was transported multiple times to the hospital. One of my fondest memories is when he was able to come home after his first one hundred days in the hospital. CareFlite offers ground services as well as helicopter transport, and Blake was stable enough to come home by ambulance. I rode with him and watched as the team closely monitored Blake. The care from these people gave me a deep respect for everyone who works on a medical transport. Their attention to Blake was truly inspiring, especially when his oxygen numbers went down during that trip. I ended up on the floor of the ambulance with the team, making sure our son was OK. Once his oxygen returned to normal, I was able to get back up into my seat. This was just one of many instances that made me think about the seriousness of medical emergencies and how life can change so quickly.

We made priceless memories during holidays, birthdays, and our son's baby dedication. We visited the zoo and spent a weeklong getaway in a friend's cabin. We found hope in Jesus and scripture verses. People poured love and support into our lives, encouraging us on days when we didn't know if we could make it another step.

Our son lived for a little over two years. As we walked out of the hospital on the day he passed, I saw some familiar faces from CareFlite medical teams. I told them of Blake's passing. I shared with them how grateful I was that they were part of our lives and thanked them for their service. We hugged and shared warm memories.

• • •

Now, twenty years later, I still look through my journal. Blake's story and my thoughts and prayers are reminders of the beauty revealed to us during those years. I discovered that journaling left behind a trail of treasures I couldn't always see at the moment. This recording of the tapestry of our experiences created a beautiful story crafted over time.

Since then, we continue to experience beauty in different ways than we expected. As a family, we have been able to laugh and enjoy holidays again. Our pain has evolved into warm memories. And we have used our story to encourage others when things seem hopeless.

I lived through some difficult things. Difficult days will come again. But I know that in sickness and in health, there is hope of the promise found through Jesus. One thing we learned is that God makes everything beautiful in its time, a sentiment we had inscribed on Blake's headstone.

Prayer for a Hope-Filled Life

Dear God, there are days when all we see is pain, hurt, and sickness. We yearn to feel the hope found in You. Give us glimpses of hope as we walk through another day with You at our side. Amen.

He gives strength to the weary and increases the power of the weak. Even youths grow tired and weary, and young men stumble and fall; but those who hope in the LORD will renew their strength.

Isaiah 40:29–31 (NIV)

IT'S EASY TO FEEL worn down many days. Dealing with illness, spending too many hours working, caring for our loved ones, and many other responsibilities can sap our energy. Even eating the right foods and getting enough rest don't seem to help.

But there is something—Someone—who will always renew our strength: God. His offer is not like a caffeine buzz we rely on in the morning or the sugar high we reach for during corner-store visits. Those choices only provide man-made, temporary fixes to our daily exhaustion.

God's promise, like His person, is steadfast. He vows to remedy our spiritual and physical fatigue. He doesn't require us to drink protein shakes or visit the gym several times a week (though those are great for our health). All we need to do is place our hope in Him. When we do that, we are guaranteed the vitality only He can give, stronger and faster than the energy of youth. We'll be able to rise above our challenges.

As we're told in Isaiah 40:31 (NIV), "They will soar on wings like eagles; they will run and not grow weary, they will walk and not be faint." With God, we can rise above every challenge.

This isn't rocket science. It's simple faith and hope in action. We ask, He gives.

This promise is one we can depend on, no matter what draining situations we encounter. Isn't it comforting to know that God will be there to help? And isn't it wonderful to understand that when we have nothing left to give, He will carry us?

In His arms, we will walk, we will run—we'll even soar. All it takes is hope.

—Heidi Gaul

The LORD makes firm the steps of the one who delights in him.

Psalm 37:23 (NIV)

A VISION FOR MOVING FORWARD

By Eryn Lynum

THE NEW SCHOOL YEAR was here, and I felt unready and terribly unmotivated. Every back-to-school picture I saw from friends was a poignant reminder that I was behind. It seemed everyone was cheerfully heading into the new season while I sat unenthusiastic and a bit hopeless. We were several years into our homeschooling journey, yet this season felt very different. Typically, as the weather begins to turn, a chill in the air brings enthusiasm for the upcoming year. Yet, like a bird failing to return for fall migration, my annual excitement for lesson planning and charting our coming year never arrived.

On a September day, when everyone else seemed fully acclimated to the new school year, I sat in my yard feeling defeated. A question that I refused to voice hovered in my mind: *Do I really want to keep educating my children at home?* It wasn't a question of ability. My husband and I had both been raised in homeschooled homes. We'd educated our children over the past few years. I knew I could mentally and physically muscle my way through another year. What deeply concerned me was my lack of desire. No, it was not a question of whether I could do it, but did I want to.

I had seen in past years how God had been faithful to His promise in establishing our steps. I read in Psalm 37:23 (NIV), "The LORD makes firm the steps of the one who delights in him." He had always made way for us to educate our children at home. Even when funds were tight for supplies and curriculum or sickness wiped out weeks of progress, He had leveled the path and led us forward. Yet, in prior years, His preparations had always included motivation. I feared I just didn't have it in me this year.

Although this lack of enthusiasm was new to my experience as a homeschool mom, I'd experienced similar struggles in other areas of my life. I have felt it when initial enthusiasm for an endeavor wanes, and I find myself unwilling or unsure how to continue. I've even had these lackluster seasons in my faith walk. There have been times when following Jesus hasn't felt as shiny and inspiring as it did at the beginning of my journey. I long for the excitement when His Word feels fresh. There have been times when I've opened my Bible only to feel nothing new, its familiarity seeming stale.

However, God has helped me to see those times as seasons of maturation. I'm no longer fueled by the initial excitement and emotions I felt when my faith was young. Instead, I commit myself to a deeper understanding of His Word and experience His enduring hope and goodness on a new level. I'm no longer resting my faith on fickle emotions but on the firm foundation of His living and active Word. As this maturation happens, I can, as Psalm 34:8 (NIV) says, "Taste and see that the Lord is good."

• • •

Like establishing my faith steps with a desire for growth, God was giving me a new perspective for educating my children. Sitting in my yard that afternoon, I prayed, asking Him to establish the steps before me. In the coming weeks, it wasn't an excitement for arithmetic or spelling that He revived. Instead, He restored in me a vision for discipling my children. I knew that having them at home afforded countless opportunities to help them grow in their faith.

As He renewed my vision, excitement came with it. I eagerly gathered resources and planned lessons to help my children study God's Word and explore subjects around Biblical history, missionary stories, and understanding God through science and creation.

I hadn't known this was what I was praying for or what it would set in motion for coming years. Yet ever since that fall, we've viewed our homeschooling journey and, in a broader sense, our parenting path very differently. We only have our kids with us for so long, and we can harness those opportunities to point them to Jesus and strengthen their faith.

I think of this often when I ask God to establish the way before me. Whether in a writing project, a new challenge my husband and I are facing in parenting, or an opportunity on the horizon, when I ask God to establish our steps, I prayerfully prepare my heart for renewed vision. Beholding an opportunity or task, I picture myself as the fictitious woman of Proverbs 31:16 (NIV) who "considers a field and buys it; out of her earnings she plants a vineyard." I want to be one who wisely considers the opportunity before me.

I can envision a barren field and the potential its soil holds. But I don't want to set my shovel to the dirt without first praying for God's vision. In the same way, I want to know what He wants to bring forth from the coming school year. What growth does He want to cultivate in my soul? What creative endeavors does He have for me to follow through on? Where is He calling me to nurture my relationship with my husband? When I stand before these empty fields, I'm practicing trading my plans for His. He wants to bring forth a harvest far greater than I can fathom.

• • •

In surrendering my agenda, He removes distractions and fine-tunes my gaze so I can see a starting point on His path. It's much like what I experienced one day when our family visited the mountains. We stood in a valley we knew well. Yet dense fog was shrouding the landscape and obscuring familiar features and trails. I knew magnificent summits were hemming us in on every side. But on this day, the fog narrowed my attention to what was directly in front of me. I noticed the beauty of the trees, willows, and creek like never before.

Sometimes, when the way ahead is obscured by fog, God helps me see what is right in front of me, like that day in my yard when I asked Him to establish a way to teach our children. I didn't know what He was up to or what was coming. He didn't immediately lift the fog. Instead, He narrowed my gaze to the opportunities before me. He gave me a new perspective. I didn't need to plan an entire year or orchestrate impressive lessons. Instead, He was calling me to gently guide my children to Himself, and that was a vision I was excited to follow.

If I had tried to muster the motivation and plan a course merely marked by math, writing, and geography, I don't believe we would have made it through that school year. My resolve would have quickly waned, and feelings of failure would have paralyzed me. Mere academic goals and self-motivation wouldn't hold up to the challenges a school year brings. How often have I settled for a vision smaller than God has for my family and me? I can be like the Israelites under God's rebuke in Isaiah 30:1 (ESV), "'Ah, stubborn children,' declares the Lord, 'who carry out a plan, but not mine.'" I regularly feel the ache of insufficient energy, time, or resources. I'm keenly aware of my limited reserves and want to employ them in the right direction. I don't want to waste what God has given me on a plan that is not His.

That season, God knew my vision wasn't strong enough, so He gave me a much grander one. My plan wasn't purposeful enough, so He infused it with His truth and intentionality. He was interested in much more than my children's academics—He wanted to capture their hearts. In doing so, He also recaptured mine. As a result, my faith blossomed that year alongside my children's. Together, as we followed God's course and He established our steps in His truth and wonder, vision turned to reality. We found our faith rooted deeper and our hearts brimming with hope for what God has in store.

Prayer for a Hope-Filled Life

Dear God, I don't want to move forward in my limited strength. Instead, establish the way before me by granting a new perspective and a glimpse of the beauty You want to bring forth.

And now these three remain: faith, hope and love. But the greatest of these is love.

1 Corinthians 13:13 (NIV)

FAITH, HOPE, AND LOVE

By Heather Jepsen

I HAVE BEEN A SMALL-CHURCH pastor for more than sixteen years. One of the blessings of this job is getting to know wonderful people. I have served in my current position for more than ten years. This has given me lots of time to get to know people not only as members of my church, but also as personal friends.

Two of my favorite people from church are Ann and James Colton. The Coltons were pillars of our church community. They had been members for decades and were very generous with both their time and their financial resources. They were leaders in the church who attended worship every Sunday, were active on committees, and participated in Sunday school and Bible studies. Everyone knew Ann and James, and everyone loved them.

As happens so often in later life, eventually someone got sick. While on a trip, Ann began to have some strange symptoms, suggesting possible uterine cancer. They came home right away, and surgery was scheduled. Unfortunately, during Ann's surgery, doctors found that the cancer had already spread throughout her abdomen. It was stage four, and the prognosis wasn't good.

Ann was in her eighties but not ready to give up on life. For several months she tried chemotherapy, but her body could not handle the treatments. I remember at Christmas she was in the hospital, struggling to remain healthy despite the poison in her system. James had gone to see her, and he told me that on Christmas Eve they sat with a battery-operated candle singing hymns and praying. Even in her illness, Ann and James were bringing faith and hope to everyone at the hospital.

It was decided that Ann should end the treatments, so she returned home with hospice care. She had several good months and we enjoyed many visits. I would stop and pick up a pizza and we would share a lunch, sometimes just the three of us, sometimes with our families, and sometimes with Bible group members from church. Even though things weren't perfect, the generosity of Ann and James could not be stopped. They just loved to host people in their home.

• • •

One of the beautiful aspects of a slow death is that there is lots of time to talk about it and grieve before it happens. Ann, James, and I talked often about how they felt about her impending death. Always they were faithful, confident in the promise of God to see them through. They were such an inspiration to me. I left our visits uplifted realizing that if Ann could find hope in her slow and painful death experience, then I could find hope in whatever struggles I faced.

Eventually, Ann grew weaker and could no longer host company. She spent her days in bed, with James at her side. Still, church family was welcomed into their home, and they were eager to hear news of happenings from the faith community.

As Ann neared death, I was busy preparing for a mission trip to Africa. I was so worried she would die while I was overseas, but the Coltons assured me that I must go. I was the leader of the church, and they wanted me to have the experience of leading the church in mission.

In an answer to prayer, Ann held on until I returned three weeks later. She and James eagerly welcomed me, and I sat at her bedside and shared all the news of my adventures in Malawi. As Ann and James heard about our trip, they were moved to help the mission. The village we had partnered with needed fresh water, and there on her deathbed, Ann and James committed the money to build a well in that village. It would be several thousand dollars, but they were undaunted. This would be her dying gift to the church.

About a week later, the time of Ann's death arrived. Her family came from around the country, and as the moment neared, they called me to the bedside. They wanted to pray with the pastor. Together we held hands around the bed, with Ann closing the circle, and we prayed for a peaceful transition from this life to the next. In all my years of ministry, I have never witnessed a more peaceful death for both the deceased and the family. It was such a blessing, and it fills me with hope to remember it even today. God called Ann home, and it was a joy.

As we planned and prepared a funeral service, James had one special request. Would it be possible to have a champagne toast for Ann after the funeral? In my church, decisions are made by committees and not pastors, so I said I would ask.

Although as a faith community we do not encourage drinking, the leadership committee felt that a champagne toast would be a fitting tribute to Ann. This funeral was to be about love and joy, and we wanted to share and celebrate Ann's great hope and faith.

As I prepared the homily for the service I was led to the words of Paul's letter to the church in Corinth. So often used at weddings, 1 Corinthians 13 is a wonderful treatise on love within the church community. Ann had so fully shown the love of God to all she met. So patient, so kind, so faithful and joyful and loving. Ann was someone I looked up to, and I know I was not the only one to feel that way.

When the day of the service came, the church was full to the rafters. We all were so happy to celebrate Ann, and yet our hearts ached at her death. Her son sang a moving tribute, and I could feel the tears begin to stream down my face. It is so hard to lead a funeral service for someone you love. And truly I had loved Ann, as she had shown the love and generosity of God to so many.

I pulled myself together, dried my eyes, and gave the homily. Yes, the congregation seemed to reply. Ann was the epitome of the love of God. So hopeful, so generous, so full of kindness and compassion. She was just one of those special people.

We went downstairs into our fellowship hall and out came the champagne glasses. Nothing fancy, mind you, just plastic stemware, but the bottles were passed around and everyone had a small pour. I called the group to attention and James led the cheer. "To Ann, who taught us God's faith, hope, and love! Hip hip hooray!"

Time passed and James kept coming to church. He and I stayed in touch, and I still regularly visited his house as he moved through the stages of grief. Even when you know someone is dying, it is different when they are gone.

Two years after Ann's death, my church returned to Africa. We visited our village in Malawi, and there we saw the clean water well that had been funded with Ann's generous dying gift. To my wonder and surprise, the people of the village had carved Ann's name in the cement: "Clean water, a blessing from God, and from Ann Colton." My eyes filled with tears. Even though she had long passed, Ann's faith and generosity were still making an impact the world over.

• • •

Many years have passed since the death of Ann Colton. James is still alive but has moved into a care facility two hours away. He and I still talk on the phone now and then, but our relationship has changed. The church has changed too, as they always do. Many new people have come who don't remember Ann and James. But even today, as we discuss great saints and inspiring people, Ann's name will come up in a Bible study or Sunday school class. Such was the impact of her kindness, faith, and hope.

The biggest lesson I learned from Ann was how to die. Death is a part of our world, and we know it is something we cannot avoid. Thankfully, in our faith, we believe that death is not the end. Even though Ann had a long and drawn-out death, she never complained. Right up to her last breath she was so peaceful and so hopeful. She was such a testament to faith. She knew she was with God, and she knew she would be with God after she died. Her quiet resolve meant more to me than anything else. And it enabled me to minister to others in their moments of death in a new and profound way. Hope in the face of death is the greatest gift of our faith.

Prayer for a Hope-Filled Life

Gracious God, may my life be filled with faith, hope, and love. In every moment of every day, may I show kindness, generosity, and love to Your world. Amen.

He will wipe every tear from their eyes. There will be no more death or mourning or crying or pain, for the old order of things has passed away.

Revelation 21:4 (NIV)

SORROW IS AN EMOTION each of us has likely experienced at some point in life. Pain, regret, and guilt are also familiar emotions that may have pierced our hearts. Sometimes these wounds are so deep that it seems even time won't heal them.

Although it isn't always easy, we can learn from—and in some ways, turn from—the past. This doesn't mean ignoring our circumstances or pretending we're OK when we're not. It means turning to Jesus.

When we look to a future in heaven, we see a place of joy and peace, a place where love reigns forever. There is no more crying, no more grief or hurt or pain. And we can trust this is our future because Jesus told us so. But how can we apply our knowledge of the perfect happiness awaiting us to our less-than-perfect present? Is there a way to soften the hurt for now?

In short, yes! Like a child who has fallen and skinned a knee, our soul aches for the comfort of a parent's kiss. That simple act of love that helps the little one forget the momentary hurt so he can once again run and play is the same simple act of love we receive from the Father that allows us to move forward every day. God sees our pain and understands our agony. He will hold us close for as long as we need and let us run free when we are once again ready.

Each of us bears scars, and we're all in different stages of healing. But we can have hope that every one of our hurts will mend, completely and permanently. While the world we live in is flawed, the one we are going to is not. It will be just as perfect as a hug and a promise from our Father, as He wipes every tear from our eyes.

—Heidi Gaul

Trust in the LORD with all your heart, and lean not on your own understanding; In all your ways acknowledge Him, and He will shall direct your paths.

Proverbs 3:5–6 (NKJV)

JOY IN THE MORNING

By Elsa Kok Colopy

THE HOT WATER WRAPPED my body like a heated blanket. I sank lower in the tub to let its warmth fully envelop me. Hot tears spilled out of my eyes, down my cheeks, and into the water. It'd been a good few decades since I'd had an ugly cry like this one—sobs heaving through my chest and strange sorrowful sounds slipping from my mouth.

He was gone.

My little boy was gone.

No, he hadn't died, though it felt a little like he had. Laurentz had been taken from the orphanage by his teenage birth mom. We'd been in the process of adopting him for almost three years, and the paperwork was nearly completed. He was supposed to be coming home within the next year. We'd been visiting him every quarter and had grown deeply attached, imagining a forever life together with our son. His young mom had wanted the adoption, as she had neither the means nor the ability to care for Laurentz in the dangerous city where she lived. That, and she said she truly wanted to give him every opportunity for a safe and love-filled life. Understandably, her heart was also torn. And now she had decided she just couldn't go through with it.

• • •

I took a few deep, shaky breaths and tried to stem the tears. "God," I whispered, "I just can't imagine life without him! I trust You, I really do. If we are meant to support Laurentz there, if we need to let him go, then please, please help my heart. Stop the flow of tears. Give us a vision for loving him from afar, for supporting him and his mom, even as we are here. We are willing, Lord. If that is what's best, we are willing. Just please, give me the courage to accept it."

Later that evening, as I lay spent and worn in my bed, my phone dinged. I glanced down, tears still clouding my eyes. It was a text from a close friend. "Psalm 30:5 (CEV). For you, my friend. 'At night we may cry, but when morning comes we will celebrate.'"

The verse seared my heart, as verses sometimes do. I felt God's warmth through it. And yet I wanted more details.

Would rejoicing come because our son would return? Or would rejoicing come as we let him go and supported him and his mom in Haiti? I couldn't imagine the latter—not with the danger in the streets and the deep famines. Would Laurentz even survive? The emotion flooded my heart once again. The touch of warmth whisked away by worry and fear.

The next morning, I crawled out of bed and went to my spot at the table. I wearily cracked open my journal and grabbed my Bible. Again, tears. I wiped them away and tried to focus on the scriptures I'd just opened up to. One sentence popped out to me.

Psalm 30:5. "At night we may cry, but when morning comes we will celebrate."

My eyes opened wide. The exact verse my friend had texted me the night before. This time, my eyes focused on one word: *will.* "When morning comes we *will* celebrate." I felt God's strong comfort wrap around my heart. "We *will* celebrate." Whatever the outcome of our adoption, God had us. He would not let us go. He would not let my husband and me go, He would not let Laurentz go. He would not let his birth mom go. And in the midst of it all, we would celebrate.

I wiped my tears. I sat up straighter. *Whatever comes*, I repeated to myself.

• • •

Just a few weeks later, the plane touched down in Haiti and we were once again at the orphanage. We had planned to adopt three children from there, so we now spent time with our special-needs son and our older daughter. Laurentz's absence was felt deeply, but there remained the hope of what God had spoken.

I was playing with Wilna, our older daughter, when word came that Laurentz's mom had come to the orphanage. We weren't allowed contact with the birth family, a protective measure for those vulnerable young women, so I sent the orphanage director to speak with her. I wanted her to know that we harbored no ill feelings, that we wanted what was best for Laurentz and we'd do all we could to help her as she parented him. I felt peace about it. I knew it was the right thing.

I heard him coming before I saw him. Those familiar little footsteps came running up behind me. I turned and even as I opened my arms, Laurentz was already in them, hugging me close and nestling in. The orphanage director wasn't far behind. "She wants you to adopt him," she said. "She wants him to be part of your family."

Tears again. This time tears of joy. My son wrapped his arms around me and kissed my cheek. We held each other close.

Even as we held each other, I was achingly aware of a young mom whose heart was filled with sorrow. She knew he would be safe with us, but that didn't mean her heart wasn't breaking as she let him go. I committed in my heart and to the little boy in my arms that he would know and love his mom—as long as we had anything to do with it.

• • •

Six years later, I walk by Laurentz sitting at the kitchen table. His birth mom is on FaceTime and I stop to wave and smile. "How are you?" I ask.

"I'm good," she says, having worked hard to learn the English language. "Happy to see him getting so tall!"

"I know, right? He's shooting up!"

I leave them to their chat and make my way upstairs. I glance back at my strapping young son talking to his beautiful birth mom. I hear his clear, strong voice and know that nutrition and education and love have served him well. I see him treating his birth mom with love and respect, and I know his growing faith, taught in our home, has served him well also. I see his smiling mama grinning at him with pride through the iPad—and I suddenly remember the verse God gave me.

"We will celebrate."

Well, we did celebrate. And joy is here.

To stay.

Prayer for a Hope-Filled Life

Dear Jesus, help me to fully trust in You as I live this life. I have such specific ways I think things should unfold, but I know You have a way that's best for me beyond what I can even imagine. Help me to hold fast to You!

Rejoice always, pray continually, give thanks in all circumstances; for this is God's will for you in Christ Jesus.

1 Thessalonians 5:16–18 (NIV)

HOPE-FILLED PRAYERS

By Bettie Boswell

STANDING IN THE FERTILE field, I stretched my back and looked at the rows of mounded soil. Spring warmth washed over my shoulders. Birds chirped in the distance. The fragrance of blossoming trees filled the air. God had blessed my world and I gave thanks for His goodness. I looked forward to a season of growth. I thought that growth would be in the form of fresh vegetables and fruits. I had no idea what lay ahead in the coming days.

• • •

I'd spent the morning planting seeds and tending to my two young sons. I prayed for both the sown seeds and our children as I worked. My boys played in a little red wagon most of the time. Their attempts to help with the planting were mostly amusing, but I hoped they enjoyed the time we spent together as much as I did. Kindergarten would come all too soon for the oldest. My younger son had just started saying a few words, though he seemed to understand everything we said.

I enjoyed being a full-time mom. Having a garden each year helped reduce the effect of monthly grocery bills. I'd also acquired a few piano students to supplement my husband's income as a minister. Budgets were tight, but staying home with my children felt like the right choice.

Sunday arrived the following day with another bright springtime feeling in the air. I prayed with my young class of preschool students during Sunday school and read them a Bible story. We sang songs of praise before heading to worship. Our church had no children's activities during services so I always had a supply of snacks to keep my boys quiet during worship. They usually finished their pack of goodies around the sermon's end. There were several rotating pianists in the congregation, so when it was my turn to play I would hand my snacks over to a sweet older woman. When that happened, I prayed and hoped the boys would make it through the song service without a cry for me or my husband.

• • •

Church services proceeded as usual that Sunday with songs and a sermon. After the final chorus, most of the congregation walked outdoors to visit in the warm sunshine. Several spouses, including my husband, stayed inside the building for a board meeting so fellowship lasted longer that day. Some of the women seemed more affectionate than usual as we chatted and chased children together. They were a friendly bunch but something seemed different as the leadership meeting time lengthened. No one had mentioned anything amiss, but my curiosity grew and I prayed that all was going well.

Then my husband walked from the building. The expression on his face told me there was a problem. After we got home, he shared the news that he no longer had a job. The board felt that five years was long enough to serve their congregation. The bottom dropped out of my world.

Tears poured from my eyes. I'd made up my mind that we would someday move out of the parsonage, have our own home, and be permanent residents of the area. That dream would no longer be a possibility. Looking around the home where our children had lived for all their young lives, and knowing we had to leave, broke my heart. When my babies came from their playroom, I had no choice but to be a pleasant mom, at least on the outside.

For several days, my husband and I alternately prayed for answers and ranted about what had happened. Our prayers seemed to go unanswered. Not only would we be without an income in a matter of months, we would be homeless if something didn't change soon. I watched the seeds I'd planted in the patch behind the parsonage sprout and start to grow. Someone else would reap the harvest I'd planted with my children. I wanted to go out and hoe every growing plant down. Despair filled my heart over the next few weeks as I watched letters of application go out and letters of rejection return. We dismissed thoughts of trying to find a job for me, knowing we wouldn't be living in that location anymore.

• • •

One morning, before my family arose from sleep, I fell to my knees and cried out to God with all my heart. We only had a few more weeks to be in the parsonage. Time was running out. I'd been praying all along, but this time all the anguish that had built up inside me poured out as I begged God to help us in our time of need. A glimmer of hope filled my heart as I fought against doubts threatening to overwhelm me. I trusted God and knew He would lead us where He wanted us to be, but I was scared. I kept praying until my worries were defeated.

It didn't take long for the Lord to answer my desperate petition. Within the next few days we had positive responses from two churches who wanted us to come meet their respective congregations. One was in a northeast metropolitan area and another in a southern town. Knowing we finally had choices gave me hope. The prospect of moving from the place that had once felt like a forever home now seemed like a release instead of a sorrowful regret. My father-in-law had connections with moving companies and promised to help us relocate to a new church or back to my husband's hometown, a few hours away. God had answered my prayer abundantly.

My in-laws came to watch our children as my husband and I flew north and then south to explore new possibilities.

After our whirlwind trips it became clear which location would best suit our family. We accepted the invitation to serve the church in a family-friendly southern town. We began packing in earnest. We had no idea where we would live because the church didn't have a parsonage. We traveled together as a family to our new town and met with a real estate agent. We had hopes of finally living in a home of our own, even if we had to rent something.

Thankfully, God also solved that dilemma with an answer to prayer. He provided my parents with an unexpected windfall, and they gave us enough money to put a down payment on a house. Our new town had a university where I could take classes for teacher certification. That career would still give me abundant time to be with my children during their growing years.

That day when I'd planted the seeds behind the parsonage, I had no idea what kind of growth would take place. Instead of seeing those seedlings grow, I saw my relationship with God grow in my prayer life and also in my trust in Him to know that my family and I would survive these changes and learn from them. Through it all, God watched out for my family and gave us hope of better days.

Prayer for a Hope-Filled Life

Dear Lord, when I pray, help me to realize You are able to do the impossible. In all things, increase my trust in Your hope for the future. In Jesus's name, Amen.

Yet you are enthroned as the Holy One; you are the one Israel praises.

Psalm 22:3 (NIV)

SAYING THANK YOU TO LIFE

By Roberta Messner

I PRESSED THE DOORBELL at the brick rancher on Oak Lane. The neighborhood was abloom with pink and white dogwoods. But I was heartsick. I had lost touch with my nurse-friend Kay. Now she was gone.

I'd been summoned here by her brother Mel, the administrator of her estate. How many times I'd sat with Kay in her cozy home with more questions than answers about the illness I'd lived with since childhood. The tumors, the pain, the surgeries that never ended. Kay's lupus affected every system of her body, yet she never seemed to doubt like I did. Her faith in God's plan for her life—her hope—were rock-solid. I tried to pretend I had it all together. When the mask got too heavy, I invented excuses to stay away.

From Mel I'd learned that Kay had passed the month before. The latest assault on her body had been a leg amputation. We'd never get to have the conversation about the strength that sustained her. If there was ever an angel who walked this Earth, it was Kay. But what did Mel want with *me*? "Can you come at two, Roberta?" he'd asked in the official-looking letter mailed in a long white business envelope. "I'd like to talk with you about my sister, and I also have something for you."

Mel answered the door right away. "Roberta?" he said. "Come in, come in. I've heard a lot about you over the years." He stationed himself in a folding chair in front of a table with paperwork scattered about, and invited me to have a seat.

I liked Mel immediately and shared with him my first memory of Kay. How we'd met in the linen closet of the VA hospital when I was a new nurse and Kay a seasoned ICU staffer. "Anything you need, I'm just down the hall," she assured me. "These veterans are a special lot. No question is too big or too small to help them out."

As time went on, Kay and I saw each other outside of work. Neither of us had children, so there was time for long, chatty dinners and concerts. I didn't cook much, so Kay gifted me with goodies from her kitchen. I created decorative accents for her.

Nothing could have prepared me for being in Kay's home again. On the plush celery-green carpet I'd once helped her select were small groupings of objects. I saw a towering stack of Pampered Chef products earmarked for Laurie, a new bride at Kay's church. One designated

"Roberta" was in a corner by the fireplace. Seeing the question mark on my face, Mel explained, "Kay wanted you to have these. Some are presents I believe you once gave her. Others...." His warm voice trailed off.

• • •

She left me *something?*

I noticed a sampler I'd once sewn for her. It featured two young girls reading storybooks on a window seat. Underneath were the words "Cherish Each Golden Hour." There was an antique cake plate, a purse. Mel retreated to his chair. "Kay didn't want us to have an estate sale," he said softly. "She tagged everything with a special one's name on it before she went to heaven. To thank them for all they'd meant to her."

Still perplexed, I fingered the purse, a red pebbled-leather doctor's satchel I'd bought when we worked together as nurses. Kay's dear handwriting tucked inside the wintergreen-scented pouch told the story:

> *Dear Roberta,*
>
> *I'll never forget the day you gave me this. You'd saved up to buy it for yourself. It was on the chair in your living room when I stopped by. Red! Your favorite color.*
>
> *I'd never realized how much I liked red. You flew off to your kitchen for a paper sack from Big Bear and began unloading everything. I wanted to tell you to*

stop, but I couldn't get the words out. To think I'd be carrying that purse!

Thank you, Roberta. I've loved it all this time. It's yours again. Always remember: It's friends who are the real riches.

Love,

Kay

I swiped my eyes with the sleeve of my blue-striped shirt. The cake plate brought back another memory. Kay had taped her recipe for my pick of her baked goods: cranberry cornucopia cake. The card was splotched with a butter stain, on the reverse side another note.

Remember when I made a hundred of these that Thanksgiving? Taking them around was so much fun. On my walk to everyone's door I thanked God for putting those friends in my life. My favorite of all was the one I brought to you. They'd removed the big tumor behind your eye. You put on a pot of coffee and we sat on your porch swing for an hour. I've smiled every time I've thought of it.

That hadn't been all. Kay had prepared a six-course, almond-crusted chicken dinner she delivered from her car, complete with a tasty sorbet palate cleanser. She brought along iced tea with real peach slices and mint, and a carafe of French vanilla coffee to have with the cake. She ate with me at the round oak table in my kitchen. Then out on the swing she prayed the loveliest prayer for my recovery, closing with words from Philippians 1:3 (CSB): "I give thanks to my God for every remembrance of *Roberta*."

No one but Kay had ever replaced a *you* in Scripture with my name.

Atop the crystal pedestal cake plate was still another note:

> *You loved this, Roberta. I've always regretted not giving it to you that day. There's no time like the present for presents of the heart. Nor for saying thank you to those we hold dear.*

Mel handed a jeweler's ring box to me. "She wanted you to have this too," he said. Inside the velvet box was the delicate diamond Kay had worn on the itty-bitty finger ravaged from her connective tissue disorder. Inserted in the slit holding the ring was a square of folded yellow paper. I read her words slowly, then with blurred vision, assigning them to a forever place in my heart.

> *Thank you for our friendship, Roberta. Even when we didn't see each other, I felt you with me, especially when I thanked God for you. When we thank Him, He always shows up. Gives us hope for whatever's ahead. Will you make every moment Thanksgiving too?*
>
> *Love always,*
> *Kay*

• • •

The ring was much too small to fit my own finger, so I had it made into a charm for my memory bracelet. I wear it every day, whether with jeans or dressing up. When a nurse at one of the hospitals complimented me on it, I pointed to the diamond charm that nudged me to a new way of living. "Kay was one of my patients," the lady said. "Unforgettable! When she had the leg amputation, she didn't focus on what she'd lost, but what was still hers." The nurse told of an evening when Kay's call light buzzed. She wasn't asking for help, just wanted all the staff to come to her room when they had a moment. They circled her bed. One by one, Kay thanked them for the specific ways they had cared for her.

She had lived and died with gratitude on her lips.

I often think how Kay could've had the estate sale to end all estate sales. As her way of saying "thank you" to life, she chose to give it all away. In doing so, her final gift was the passing on of her hope.

"Cherish each golden hour." I'd once stitched those words on a sampler. I would begin to live them. It would start with a grateful heart.

Prayer for a Hope-Filled Life

God of all hope, wherever gratitude resides,
You are there. Thank You.

But we know that when Christ appears, we shall be like him, for we shall see him as he is. All who have this hope in him purify themselves, just as he is pure.

1 John 3:2–3 (NIV)

FOR MANY OF US, childhood represents a time of endless adventure, a place in which we gained new skills. The world stretched before us, inviting us to learn and grow. We spent our time watching—and attempting to match—the abilities of those we admired most. If you're like me, you might have spent your days trailing after an older sibling or friend, learning valuable life lessons and meeting fresh goals.

As children of God, we want to resemble Jesus. In the Bible, we read of His love, His wisdom, and His serving nature. We are eager learn from Him, to follow in His footsteps, and to live in a way that honors Him. God's will for us is lived out in humility and grace. At times, we might encounter challenges, but as Jesus refines our souls and our faith matures, discernment becomes second nature to us. The temptations we've faced in the past lose their hold over us. Our faith strengthens us, and our nature comes to reflect Jesus more clearly. We are growing toward His likeness, becoming recognizable as part of His family.

When we study the faces of our brothers and sisters in Christ, we might spot a special physical element or a demeanor that marks them as different. Whether we see it in a gentle smile or in the way they carry themselves with humble confidence, it's there. It's the inherent mark of Jesus in our spiritual DNA. Love, joy, and peace—the fruits of the spirit are evident in all believers as we go about our day-to-day routines. As John stated in 1 John, we can trust that when Jesus again appears, we will be like Him. Until that day, we can live in hope, purifying ourselves just as He is pure.

Can anything be more thrilling than knowing we will someday be like Jesus? Can any hope be greater? This is our future—eternal, bright, and beautiful. We will be purified children of God, recognizable inside and out.

—Heidi Gaul

And we know that in all things God works for the good of those who love him, who have been called according to his purpose.

Romans 8:28 (NIV)

AN UNEXPECTED PATH TO PERSONAL HEALING

By Cristina Moore

I REMEMBER THE DAY that started my husband and me on the path that led us to face our PTSD. Looking back, it seems unfathomable that I almost walked away from taking the first steps that would lead to a successful business and partnership, life-changing projects, and an unexpected answer to prayer, providing hope for not only our business but to our personal healing.

That day, I'd sat across from John, one of the founders of Purple Heart Homes, a nonprofit whose mission is to provide housing solutions for disabled and aging veterans.

I had met John more than eight years before, when I became a founding board member as he and his partner Dale launched their charity.

• • •

I learned a long time ago that when John called, I answered. He was always looking for ways to better the lives of veterans who had fought in all wars, not just Afghanistan and Iraq. I was a bit distracted when we met. My husband had recently left his job and I was deep in worry about him finding a new one and how long we could live off our savings.

I'd absently listened to John's request while I played with the wrapper from my straw and waited for our food to arrive. We moved through the normal small talk quickly since he was clearly anxious to share his proposal. My "no" answer was on my lips in response to his request for me to start a for-profit arm of his charity focused on building manufactured homes. He shared that both he and Dale had dreamed of building villages for homeless veterans that enabled them to live in a community with support services and a safe space to heal and thrive. His voice brought me back into focus when he asked me—rather forcefully, I might add—to listen before I immediately said "no." The conversation quickly gained my full attention.

As John shared his vision for leveraging a facility the nonprofit had recently purchased to support their mission of providing housing solutions, I started to visualize his dream. He thought I would be the right person to start and lead this team given my background in lean manufacturing, construction, and leadership. John went on to say he needed someone who he could trust to implement processes in manufacturing and with the dedication to make his dream a reality.

I had all the excuses in my mind: I am too busy, our twin seven-year-olds take too much of my time, I can't add yet another job to my already busy civilian career and national guard job. The list went on. I had plenty of reasons to say no and could not find one reason to say yes—this was his dream, not mine. Simply put, I had enough activity in my life and didn't need to add anything else to it. All those protests froze in the back of my throat as I heard a small voice whisper in my mind that Rob didn't need to find a job—it found him. I looked at John and answered with "Why me? Why not Rob?"

• • •

My husband, Rob, and I met in the military while attending the officer basic course in Fort Leonard Wood, Missouri. This is where engineer officers in the army learned the basic skills needed to perform as a construction engineer—build roadways and buildings—as well as a combat engineer—build and detonate explosive devices. I served five years on active duty and then transitioned to serving in the guard, where I supported a state mission but also remained ready to support our federal mission. Rob joined the national guard with me when we settled in our new home, and we continued to serve together until his retirement in 2010.

After conducting rescue operations at ground zero in New York City after 9/11, our lives never seemed to have a dull moment or slow down. Rob deployed to Iraq from 2003 to 2004, and immediately following, we deployed together from 2004 to 2005. It was unheard of for a married couple to deploy together, let alone in the same unit. We came home safely from that mission, then Rob returned to combat in 2009 in Afghanistan while I remained at home pregnant with our twin girls. In his civilian career, Rob had worked in commercial construction as an engineer. In his military career, he served as both a combat and construction engineer. Although John only knew of Rob in passing, I knew in my heart that he was the one John needed to lead this business, not me.

Rob had transitioned as well as can be expected after his multiple earlier combat deployments. He returned home to excellent roles in his company, oftentimes including a promotion. He had transitioned from one company to another and was highly sought after for his engineering skills. His last deployment was different. *He* was different.

The week before my meeting with John, Rob had called me from his job and said he was coming home and couldn't go back. He hadn't been fired or terminated, and on the surface, the events of the day didn't seem that significant. He had gotten into a disagreement with his boss and recognized that although he'd kept his calm, his desire was to respond in absolute rage. He knew he couldn't put himself back in a situation where there was risk those thoughts would enter his mind. I understood. I had previously brought friends I cared for to tears when I had an inexplicable rage response for a simple mistake. Rob and I have since come to recognize this as trauma from our deployments. But recognition didn't mean we knew how to fix it.

As I asked John why not Rob, I wondered if this was God sending a lifeline and helping us find a new path for Rob that would leverage his talents to help veterans who shared a common background with him. John and I continued to talk and we agreed to meet again after I'd talked to Rob and gauged his interest.

Rob initially resisted, feeling like he had to find another corporate job to help provide for the family and that this proposal carried too much risk. The "no" was as quick to come to his lips as it had been for me when I first heard the proposal. I found myself working to convince him, to share with him that the timing of this offer could not be coincidence. I believed it was ordained by God. At the time, I was further in my path to building a relationship with God than Rob. I know he still struggled with believing that God cared about our lives. He eventually said yes because he knew what it meant to me and trusted my belief.

We called John back and accepted the proposal. We still didn't have the answers and had no idea how we were going to fund or start this company; we simply took a leap of faith. We both believed that the timing was not coincidence, but rather that God was guiding us to His purpose. This leap of faith led to Rob finding a new battle buddy, our partner John, who understood all that Rob had encountered because he'd had similar experiences. It also led to John finding not only a partner but also a dear friend in Rob after losing his own battle buddy and co-founder as a result of complications from his combat injuries.

We started building ramps to provide accessibility and mobility for our veterans, which quickly grew to us providing bathroom and bedroom additions. When we reached points in our business in which we no longer had personal funds to keep the business operational, our hope was renewed through unexpected grants and donations. How could we walk away or quit when so many believed in what we were doing? How could we stop when God continued to open doors?

Little did we know that while we were focusing on providing life-changing projects to veterans, we also were walking down a path to our personal healing. With every project, we were filled with renewed purpose. With every project, our network of military with similar experiences grew. With every project, a little bit of the rage continued to chip away. We were no longer alone in our battle against our demons. John's simple ask hadn't resulted in just starting a business; it resulted in us giving hope to veterans whose hope was lost...including our own.

Prayer for a Hope-Filled Life

Lord, help me to discern Your direction and follow Your path when You open doors to opportunities I may not see.

Be joyful in hope, patient in affliction, and faithful in prayer.

Romans 12:12 (NIV)

FINDING HOPE IN THE WAITING

By Amanda Hayhurst

"THERE HAVE BEEN OVER 100,000 referrals for child neglect this year just in our state alone," the presenter stated. My church was offering a class to learn more about the fostering process, so I decided to sign up. I was living in the largest county in Georgia, and the need for foster families seemed infinite. My heart broke for the children around me who had no safe place to sleep at night, while I had two extra bedrooms that sat empty. I longed to do something to help.

My husband, Marcus, and I worked full time. Our calendar was packed with social events and activities for our two boys. This girl's plate was definitely full. But even with an overwhelmed schedule, my soul felt underwhelmed. I was a follower of Jesus but felt like I was missing something. Weeks earlier I had gotten to a place where I even blurted out to God, *Whatever you call me to, I'll do it. I just want to be obedient.*

And now, no matter how much I'd tried, I couldn't shake this deep desire to give a child in need a loving, Christ-centered home. "Babe, what do you think about possibly fostering? There is such a need for it," I said to my husband. We were just leaving the presentation at church, so if any time were a good one, this was it.

"I don't know. I mean, we are so busy already. Maybe one day. But definitely not any time soon," he said.

Ugh, not the response I was hoping for. I was longing for something I knew just wasn't a reality at the time. I tried to transfer my excitement onto him but it wasn't happening. I couldn't convince my husband to be as convinced as I was. That would take the work of something supernatural. I felt helpless, so I put my desires on a shelf and started praying. I prayed that if it was God's will, He would open my husband up to the idea more. And I prayed for an abundance of patience in this frustrating place of waiting.

• • •

Over the course of a few months, God put my teenage cousin, Ivey, on my heart. I had always adored her and her beautiful sisters. I'm a boy mom, and while I love it, I have a special place in my heart for girls. I always thought how special it would be to have a built-in best friend in a daughter. Just like me and my mom were. Similar interests, spa days, girl talk. The whole shebang. But it hadn't turned out that way.

Puzzled by this prompt to pray for my cousin, I began, *God, hold this sweet girl close. Keep her safe. And lavish her in Your love.* Week after week, He reminded me to pray, quietly whispering hope into my heart. I found comfort in these weekly prayers, unsure why I was actually praying them in the first place.

Later that summer, I felt a nudge to invite Ivey down from Indiana for a few weeks. She and her sisters were temporarily living with my grandma after being removed from their home. We couldn't wait to see her and spoil her for a few weeks. She would be joining us on our yearly beach vacation to South Carolina, full of pool days, bodyboarding, and riding our bikes to the local seafood shacks and ice cream shops. Something we looked forward to every year.

"Kids, hurry up!" I yelled as we tossed the last bit of luggage into the SUV. With Ivey situated in the back seat, we were headed north to the beautiful beaches of our beloved Hilton Head. Mile after mile, my sweet cousin opened up about the rocky year she'd had. I couldn't help but glance over at my husband, who was pointedly growing in curiosity.

"Wow, I can't imagine being taken from your home like that," Marcus said. "I'm so sorry." The closer we got to the beach, the softer his heart became, his eyes periodically glancing in the rearview mirror to Ivey. Those five hours tightly packed in our family SUV were some special ones—laughing, connecting, and making memories on the road listening to our favorite music.

After arriving and unloading the car, we ran down to the beach. Approaching the rippling waves and white sandy beaches, Ivey's big blue eyes lit up. "This is amazing!"

she hollered. Seeing the familiar beaches and boardwalks through her eyes brought us back to the very first time we saw them. Her genuine gratitude and sense of wonderment was contagious. We hit the waves, each proudly holding our bodyboards over our heads and jumping into the foamy water. We biked to all our favorite spots, making sure Ivey got to see all the hidden gems we had discovered throughout the years. She fit right in.

A few days into our trip, Marcus and I woke up before the kids to watch the sunrise over the Atlantic. Sipping my coffee, I gazed upon the rising sun casting a rosy hue in the morning sky. My husband leaned over, placing his hand on mine, "What do you think about inviting Ivey to stay with us?" he whispered. Wiping my teary eyes on my sleeve, I nodded yes, gently smiling back at him.

• • •

Just weeks after returning home, we became Ivey's legal guardians. Living together, we quickly learned how much we had in common. Our love for singing and cooking. Laughing over the same goofy things. And our oddly similar mannerisms. I was beginning to have my own little built-in best friend. That special place in my heart for girls was full to the brim.

During her time with us, we watched Ivey grow spiritually, finding healing from years of trauma. Early one morning before school, Ivey screamed for me to come downstairs. Startled, I ran to see what was wrong. "Amanda,

I want to get baptized. I don't want to wait any longer!" she exclaimed. Baptizing her at my friend's pool with our loved ones gathered around was a moment I'll never forget.

Although not in the timing I had in mind, God brought a child in need of love into our home when we were ready... when Marcus and I were both ready. Not every day has been easy or perfect. But what was perfect was God's timing. He had a perfect way of fulfilling the hope He placed in my heart. It was only my job to be obedient and pray.

Prayer for a Hope-Filled Life

Father, I pray for patience today as I learn to trust Your perfect timing. While I wait, help me be obedient to what You've called me to today.

"For I know the plans I have for you," says the LORD. "They are plans for good and not for disaster, to give you a future and a hope."

Jeremiah 29:11 (NLT)

HE HAS A GOOD PLAN

By Emily Carol Marszalek

AS THE DAUGHTER OF A Vietnam veteran and a proud American, the desire to serve my country was deep-rooted from a young age. I was thus thrilled to discover the Reserve Officers' Training Corp (ROTC) program that allowed participants to earn their college degree while training to be an army officer. Upon college graduation and successful completion of the four-year program, one would commission as a second lieutenant and commence service in the United States Army. I applied to the program my junior year of high school and was delighted to receive a full-ride scholarship and admittance to the program one year later.

Through a great deal of hard work, painful growth, and a massive dose of God's grace, I was highly successful in the program. I ranked number one in my class all four years: a cumulative ranking based on academics, physical fitness, and leadership. As a result of my achievements, I was allotted a host of magnificent opportunities. Twice I traveled to the United States Military Academy at West Point to participate in prestigious conferences, one of which I was the first from my university to ever garner an invitation. I was privileged to embark on a humanitarian deployment to Thailand, helping teach English to low-income children in Bangkok. The summer before my senior year, I completed an internship with an Apache helicopter unit at Camp Humphreys in South Korea, learning what it was like to be an active-duty soldier.

At the conclusion of that summer internship, I rejoiced to learn I had been placed with the Military Intelligence Corps. I was more exhilarated than ever to finish my final year and graduate with my B.A. in International Studies, commission, then head directly to Fort Huachuca, Arizona, for the Military Intelligence Basic Officer Leader Course. My promising career as a military intelligence officer was about to ignite.

When I began suffering medical problems during my senior year, I concealed my struggles for fear that the army would discard me and my career would be sacrificed. I hoped I would get better on my own. As the months progressed, however, my health rapidly declined. Eventually, I could no longer attend class or ROTC training and was hospitalized for two weeks. The health challenges I sought to hide were now evident to all. My commissioning was put on hold and I faced an army medical board. They determined I was not fit to serve.

"You will never serve in the United States Armed Forces," said the captain who delivered the news. Those ten words cut deep. I felt I had lost everything. I went from being number one in my class, esteemed by instructors and peers alike with a rewarding career at my fingertips, to nothing and no one—or so I felt. My career plans were shattered, and my heart broken.

• • •

Having grown up in a Christian household and having fostered a love of the Bible, I knew Jeremiah 29:11 well, which reminded me that God has good plans for my life. I wish I could say I immediately gleaned hope from that promise, but I didn't. The words were easy to believe when I could see the "good plans" before my eyes. Now I could see no future at all, let alone a good one.

I began to have a crisis of faith. *Had I heard God wrong?* I asked myself. *Was I not supposed to join ROTC? Were the last four years a complete waste? Did I screw up God's plan for my life?*

The struggle continued as I ping-ponged between jobs in my early-to-mid-twenties. I worked for a marketing firm, for a rental car agency, for the student accounts office at a local university, and in the records department of specialty medical offices. Despite my thinking the grass would be greener in another job, each one felt like a disappointment; I felt like a disappointment.

I eventually accepted a position working for a local university's charitable foundation. While the job was certainly not without its frustrations and challenges, I appeared to have found my niche. My hard work for the foundation was rewarded with two promotions, propelling me to an assistant director position.

During a board meeting one fall, I presented in front of foundation board members. Afterward, my supervisor relayed that a number of board members told her how impressed they were. They noted how at ease I appeared, how clearly I communicated, and my ability to genuinely engage spectators. Some of my coworkers even joked I was a professional presenter and recruited me to help them draft engaging scripts and materials for their own board presentations.

I began to think of all the times I had delivered operation orders to my peers while in ROTC, crafting and delivering orders to my squad, platoon, and battalion. It took much practice, and much failure, to learn to speak with clarity and confidence and to hone my presenting skills. Prior to ROTC, I would shake with fear and break out in a nervous sweat on my forehead at the thought of even stating my name in front of a few people.

I thought of the leadership skills I'd developed in the program too. As part of my army training, I had formulated and executed dozens of battle drills and led my unit in both field training missions and garrison operations. I'd learned how to lead a team and develop those under my supervision. I would use these leadership and management skills, refined through my experience in the program, to spearhead major foundation projects.

I began to reflect on all the jobs I'd had over the decade since I'd received that devastating news from the army. I realized that God had been gently guiding me each step of the way. In each experience and in each job, many of which I considered to be only road bumps or detours on the road I was *really* supposed to traverse, He had been fostering skills in me that I would need later on. Not a single experience was wasted. He had been coaching and growing me all along.

While working for the student accounts office, I learned how to grow a thick skin and not allow a hostile interaction with an upset customer soil my attitude and ruin my day. Working ten-hour days for the rental car agency, I learned the importance of caring for oneself outside of work and maintaining a healthy work-home balance. Working in medical offices, assisting physicians with audits and edits of their medical files, I fine-tuned attention to detail. I was also able to empathize with and encourage patients who felt discouraged by their health struggles, made possible through my own health battles.

As I reflected on each leg of my life's journey, I realized God had been coaching and growing me all along, and now He was allowing me to see that He had infused purpose into each and every step. Even when I struggled over road bumps, headed down detours, or was forced to reverse course due to an unexpected dead end, I held fast to God's promise that He has good plans for me, to give me a future and hope. Although I couldn't see a good future and didn't feel much hope all those years back when my life took such an unexpected turn, He remained faithful to His promise of good plans for my life.

Prayer for a Hope-Filled Life

Dear Lord, help me remember that even amid hardship or heartbreak, You have a good plan for my life so I can walk the path set before me full of hope and trust in You.

Consider the ravens: They do not sow or reap, they have no storeroom or barn; yet God feeds them. And how much more valuable you are than birds!

Luke 12:24 (NIV)

SMILEY FACE MAIL

By Elsa Kok Colopy

I WAS SO TIRED of worrying about money. It seemed like every time I got ahead, something would happen. My old, tired car would break down, my daughter would need something for school, or all the bills would suddenly add up to more than they did the month before. As a single mom, I'd learned to lean on God, but I wondered if my need was wearing Him out. He had supplied grocery bags of food on my doorstep, unexpected gifts under the tree at Christmas, and work that would help cover the need when it arose. But like a child nervous about asking her parents for more, I worried if there would be an end to His kindness.

"He owns the cattle on a thousand hills," my faithful friend would say to encourage my heart. "He is happy to share a few with you. You've obeyed. Now trust Him to meet you!"

My friend often reminded me of that. How when I chose to write full-time, I was obeying what God called me to do. I often bemoaned how foolish I felt not having a steady income, and she would remind me, "Steady isn't what He called you to, Elsa. He called you to trust, to hope in Him, and to watch Him work it out!"

But would He be willing to help us again? Really?

• • •

My nine-year-old daughter could sense my concern. "Mom, what's going on?"

I stood in the living room and wrapped my arms around her. She leaned into my chest. I hated when she absorbed my worry. It had been just her and me for eight years. We were so close that sometimes she felt and experienced more of my worry than I liked. "It'll be OK, Samantha. We're just about $90 short on paying rent and it's due tomorrow. I'm just not sure how we are going to cover it."

My girl pulled her head back and looked at me with her wide green eyes. "Mom, don't worry. We can pray! We'll just ask God. He promises He will take care of us, and He will!"

Oh, how I loved her childlike faith! But I also knew that God sometimes lets us go through hardships to teach us, grow us, mature us through something. While I wanted to have faith, I didn't know if He was going to provide in the way I hoped.

I nodded, wanting her faith to be founded, longing for this to be one of those times that would take root in her heart. And mine.

"OK, girl. Let's talk to Him together." I pulled her in close to me and we prayed. "God, You know what we need. We need to pay rent, and we've done everything we know to do. Will You please provide what we need? Either through work I can do tomorrow or in some unexpected way? Thank You for taking care of us. We love You!"

As I tucked my girl in to bed that night, I felt hope flood my heart. I didn't know how, but I just knew God would provide. Anticipation began to crowd out the worry. I couldn't wait to see what He would do and how He would do it. It was a warm, expectant feeling, like a child on Christmas Eve listening for Rudolph's hooves on the rooftop above—knowing good would come soon after. I crawled into my own bed, wrapped my arms snugly around my body pillow, and promptly fell asleep.

• • •

Morning dawned and with it the worry, creeping in like a shadow. I pushed it to the back of my mind. *Please, Lord.*

I walked downstairs and into the kitchen to start my morning coffee. I stood staring into the distance as the coffee gurgled through the filter. Filling a nice big mug, I added my creamer and went to sit at the kitchen table.

There it was.

The sight of it caught my breath. How did that get there? It was an envelope, leaning against our fake flower centerpiece. It had a big smiley face drawn on the outside. I quickly glanced at the sliding glass door—still locked. I looked over at the front door—also locked. Only my big brother and the landlord had a key to my place, but neither had mentioned they would be coming by, certainly not in the middle of the night.

I heard Samantha rustling upstairs and called to her. "Sam?"

She came down the steps and shuffled into the kitchen, wiping her eyes as she came. "Yes?"

"Did you put this here?" I motioned to the envelope.

She was suddenly wide awake. "That envelope? No! Did you open it? Did God send us money through smiley mail?"

I laughed out loud. "I don't know about that, honey, but let's open it and see."

I pulled the envelope off the table with shaky hands. "You open it," I said.

Samantha tore off one edge and I saw the familiar green of actual money. She pulled it out and laid each bill on the table. We counted together. "Twenty, forty, sixty, eighty—and one $10 bill. That makes..."

"Ninety!" We both said together. Our eyes were wide, goosebumps up and down our arms.

"Most people break in to steal," I said.

"But God broke in to take care of us!" Samantha laughed.

"Exactly!" We hugged each other tight as I looked to the

ceiling. "Thank You, thank You, thank You, Lord! You never fail, and You always have our back. I love You!"

"Let's thank him together," I said to my girl. And as she bowed her head, tears filled my eyes. *Thank You, Jesus.*

Prayer for a Hope-Filled Life

My good, good Father, help me to trust You to take care of me! When I feel overwhelmed by my need, help me to turn my face to You and ask for help, knowing You will be there for me.

The LORD himself goes before you and will be with you; he will never leave you nor forsake you. Do not be afraid; do not be discouraged.

Deuteronomy 31:8 (NIV)

HAVE YOU EVER BEEN afraid of being alone? Young children often are. Perhaps your own fear crept in when your children left home to start their own life or when a seemingly trustworthy friend cast you aside. Maybe a loved one's death has placed you in a situation you never wanted to be in—navigating life without someone by your side.

Yet we are never alone, as we learn in Deuteronomy. Like all of God's attributes, the quality and rarity of His steadfast devotion and protection are priceless. Knowing we can depend on Him is the cornerstone of confidence.

The Bible tells us of Ruth's decision to care for her widowed mother-in-law, Naomi. It wouldn't have been an easy choice. She could have returned to the comfort and security of her own country and dear family. Even when the older woman argued she had nothing left to give, Ruth never wavered, and she lived out her years with Naomi.

PROMISES TO YOUR LIFE

Of the many friendships described in the Bible, the one between David and Jonathan is extraordinary. At one point destined to be enemies, instead they formed an immediate friendship upon meeting. Jonathan's love for David was so deep, that his soul "was knit to the soul of David, and Jonathan loved him as his own soul" (1 Samuel 18:1, ESV). For many of us, jealousy and anger would have been our reaction to being usurped from our inherent right to the throne. Instead, Jonathan stood behind his friend. He protected David and helped him escape the enemy despite the dangerous repercussions he might face. The closeness these two shared is one of the most beautiful friendships found in the Bible.

Like Jonathan and David, through Jesus Christ and the indwelling Holy Spirit, we are now one in the spirit with God. When God states He'll never leave or forsake us, He speaks from limitless wisdom. There is no space left for fear or discouragement. He is before and behind, above and within us. His will to protect us cannot be overcome by anyone or anything.

This fact, so simple and yet so overwhelming, provides us with all we need to experience life with courage and abounding hope. We are not alone, and we never will be.

—Heidi Gaul

Let us hold unswervingly to the hope we profess, for he who promised is faithful.

Hebrews 10:23 (NIV)

BABY STEPS OF HOPE

By April Strauch

A CHURCH YOUTH GROUP all-nighter with forty teens was the last place I wanted to be. Three miscarriages and a recent diagnosis of "unexplained infertility" was all I could think about. With kids running all around me, the pressure to have fun and be encouraging was too much. I just wanted to curl up in a ball until my life made sense again.

Several months earlier my husband, Allen, suggested we volunteer to be youth leaders at our church. He said it would be good to focus on helping others rather than on the fact that we were no closer to having a family than when we began trying several years earlier.

"How ya doin'?" Sixteen-year-old Kelly flopped down at the table where I failed miserably to look interested in the twelve-hour event.

"I'm good, how are you?" My forced enthusiasm was laced with guilt. Kelly didn't seem to notice and quickly launched into her life as a sophomore in high school—homework and boys, life on a dairy farm, and her part-time job for a produce market. She made me laugh and I soon found myself wanting to get to know her better.

Soon, several other kids came over and joined in the conversation. It surprised me how they all let me in so quickly, wanted to tell me of their everyday lives. Surprisingly, by the end of the night my spirits were lifted significantly, and for the first time in days I wasn't obsessed with thoughts of our future.

• • •

Over the next couple of years, Allen and I became close to a great group of teens. Our youth group went camping, had game nights, traveled to overnight teen conventions, and hiked. Since we were the only youth leaders without children, our house soon became the hangout spot for picnics, movies, and pizza. We even enlisted the kids to help us remove an old chicken coop on our property. On more than one weekend night we spent hours talking to Kelly, Amanda, Talitha, or Nathaniel. While they told us of their ups and downs, we shared our news—we were adopting from China! They were thrilled and supported us wholeheartedly. It gave me hope that good things were coming.

Reality soon hit, though, as mounds of adoption paperwork became the new focus. Fingerprints, home studies, letters of recommendation—the sooner we gathered documents, the quicker the adoption would move forward.

Two years. That's how long our agency explained we'd have to wait to bring our baby home. By this point we'd decided to name our daughter Lily Grace. I couldn't wait to get to know her, to hold her, to be her mother. Lily would be one year old when we adopted her. The thoughts of our baby a world away, while we completed paperwork, made us impatient. During that time, I had many pregnant friends, and I envied their "short" nine months to become parents.

"We need to keep focusing on all the good God is doing in our lives," Allen told me. He was right. Weekly, we continued to enjoy the youth group. We had support from friends and family in our adoption journey. God also provided extra work for both of us with our computer business, to cover extra costs. Yet I still had days of doubting God's plan. I envied Allen, who said he felt God tell him all would be well. After the miscarriages, my heart was wounded and fragile. I wondered how I could be sure the adoption would truly come to fruition. My trust in God's plan was fading.

Through it all, we continued to be the best youth leaders we could be. I admitted to the teens that I'd never been around babies when I was young. As much as I wanted to be a mother, I was nervous. Would I do a good job? It's as if God responded to my doubts through the teens. My motherly instinct kicked in big time when Nathaniel was diagnosed with Hodgkin's disease. Walking through that season with him and his family helped me realize the depth of my capacity for caring for a young person. I didn't comprehend how much I'd truly come to care for him and his family until he was given a clean bill of health.

Allen and I often talked about the beauty of God's timing—how He allowed us to cross paths with the right kids at the right time in all our lives. Amanda, a music major, full of passion, laughingly told us one night she'd come to realize just how dramatic she could be. Kelly, a serious, pensive girl, shared how sincerely she wanted to have a better rapport with her coworker.

They truly felt like family. I learned how to care for them, planning events and meals, and giving of myself even when I thought I was too tired to keep going. I know now that God was teaching and preparing me for my own family. When I let my heart trust what God was doing and surrendered to His plan, the more hope I experienced. The moments I focused on the "whys," my impatience, doubts, and anxiety took hold. I prayed daily for faith to watch His plan unfold.

The closer we got to the two-year mark, the more excited we became. Unfortunately, the head of our adoption agency explained that due to backlogs in China, there was a chance our paperwork might expire. That would mean more time and money. He said delays happened sometimes and assured us everything was being done to speed things along.

"Don't give up hope," the agency staff told me each time I called to find out the latest. I faced a roller coaster of emotions daily, with uneasiness at the top of the list. Just when I felt I could wait no longer, the world fell apart.

It was September 11, 2001, 8:50 a.m.—Tuesday morning and a partly cloudy day. I was in my bathrobe, doing dishes when the phone rang.

It was my sister-in-law. "Turn on the TV! Now!"

It was surreal to watch the replay of the North Tower of the World Trade Center being hit by a plane. Moments later my mother called, and she and I watched as the South Tower was struck. Our eyes were glued to the TV for hours.

Somewhere around midday, my mind numb with sadness and fear, I went to the basement for a paint can. I couldn't sit still any longer. So many images of smoke, ashes, rubble, and terrified faces filled my mind. I painted the 1970s brick wall in our kitchen as my own kind of memorial for the day. I said nonstop prayers for the families who'd lost loved ones and the ones still waiting to hear. I cried as I thought of our Lily, waiting for her parents to come. After the attack, all international flights were canceled indefinitely. That day, it was hard to have faith that we'd ever hold Lily in our arms.

Three months later, while I was in the dentist's chair getting my teeth cleaned, the receptionist brought the phone to me. Allen's voice, normally calm, was hyper.

"We're going! In three days!"

I couldn't grasp what he was saying. The head of our agency had pulled strings in China and our group was scheduled to complete adoption paperwork before the government offices were closed for the Christmas season. We were finally going to be parents!

When the orphanage staff placed Lily in our arms in a faraway hotel in China, all the doubts, fears, and questions melted away. I was completely in love with my daughter. I didn't think my heart could hold any more love.

A year later, after a trip to a local amusement park with Lily's adoption group, Allen and I decided to adopt again. This time the amount of paperwork didn't get us down. Once again, we completed documents at breakneck speed and embraced the excitement of our growing family.

• • •

I guess life would be boring if things moved along without a hitch. Halfway through our second adoption, an outbreak of SARS (severe acute respiratory syndrome) in China caused more travel delays. I felt my heart tighten.

And then I heard God say to my heart: *April, I worked things out before. Can you trust Me?*

A year later, four-year-old Lily was by our side when the orphanage put baby Rayelle Anne into our arms. It was another heart-stopping, take-my-breath-away moment.

Lily and Rayelle are twenty-two and eighteen years old now. I've loved every minute of being their mother, through all the highs and lows. God has blessed me beyond my wildest dreams. I need not ever look far for hope. It's as simple as gazing into both of my daughters' eyes.

Prayer for a Hope-Filled Life

Lord, even when circumstances seem hopeless, help us trust You and wait for You to work things out in the wonderful ways that only You can.

Show them the way in which they must walk and the work they must do.

Exodus 18:20 (NKJV)

EXPANDING MY NET

By Claire McGarry

"WHAT ABOUT OFFERING just evening retreats?" my friend Jess asked, after listening to me lament about how worn out and weary I was. I'd just come back from running a weekend retreat for mothers. Its resounding success should have had me floating on cloud nine. Yet I was inexplicably exhausted. It just didn't make sense. I'd been running these retreats for years, all while raising three kids. I usually came back energized from watching how Jesus rejuvenated these women. Normally, I'd be excited to find even more ways to support moms in the trenches, and I'd be inspired to become a better mother myself. I had none of that this time. What was going on?

Sure, it took a lot of energy to pull these weekends off: arriving early at the retreat house to make all the beds, put out flowers, and place chocolates on the pillows. I wanted these women to feel cared for and pampered after spending all their time taking care of others. I even arranged for a massage therapist to come in to give massages on the first day so the women could truly unwind. I cooked all the meals and presented four faith-based sessions over the course of the three days.

Watching these women transform in Christ was what had recharged me. They typically arrived harried and wrung out after chasing kids all day, putting out fires, and battling the eternal chaos of motherhood. But after a good night's sleep, some healthy food, a few thought-provoking sessions, and quiet time to personally connect with Jesus, they became empowered. They were suddenly able to recognize the amazing work they were doing and discover the changes Jesus was prompting them to make to become even better.

• • •

This time was different. But how could I *not* provide these much-needed retreats? I'd always been blessed with an extraordinary amount of energy and thrived on being overcommitted. It fed my soul to accomplish a lot and have such a positive impact on people. I had to keep trying.

However, I realized it was taking longer and longer to recover after each retreat. Eventually, I had no choice but to go with my friend's suggestion and cut back to just evenings. It's amazing what Jesus can do in a limited period of time. Even though we had just three hours together, He still rejuvenated and renewed these women so they returned home refreshed and inspired to be great moms again.

Sadly, it was the opposite for me. After moving tables and chairs in the parish center to create private prayer spaces for each mom, running the retreat, and then putting everything back where it belonged, I was wiped out. I didn't earn enough money to pay someone else to help me. Ultimately, I'd get it all done, but my kids were paying the price. I was returning to them depleted and exhausted. That made me short-tempered and completely intolerable for the week that followed.

I felt so torn and confused. I truly believed I'd been called to lead moms to Jesus through these retreats. I'd always heard that God doesn't call the equipped; He equips the called. So why wasn't He equipping me with the energy and stamina I needed, with enough left over to be a good mother to my own children after?

Then I was diagnosed. After years and years of crazy symptoms (even once having to be carried out of an exercise class on a stretcher after just five minutes of jumping jacks), my medical team confirmed I had thoracic outlet syndrome. The skeletal makeup of my shoulders didn't allow enough room for my bones, muscles, veins, and arteries. Unbeknownst to me, every time I'd raised my arms over the years, the veins and arteries in my shoulders were being compressed between my ribs and my collarbone.

Slowly but surely, that constant hammering was building up scar tissue in a major vein, limiting the blood flow to my arms. The more I'd used my arms over the years, the more it happened. The more it happened, the more the insufficient blood flow had weakened my arm muscles.

Worse yet, when I had my arms above shoulder height for any length of time, or lifted anything heavy, the compression on that major vein would deny my heart the blood it needed. That's when subclavian steal syndrome would set in. My heart would literally steal the blood from my head. No wonder I was getting so worn out with all that housekeeping and furniture moving during those weekend and evening retreats!

My thoracic surgeon advised against the invasive surgery required to remove ribs to make more space and replace the damaged vein. Instead, he explained that, over time, my body would expand my collateral vessels, finding new paths for my blood to travel through. The blood flow would still be limited, but letting my body slowly address the issue on its own was far less risky than the surgery itself. Clearly, I had some changes to make to adapt to what was happening in my body. It was with a heavy heart that I discontinued the retreats, leaving an incredible void in my life.

• • •

I desperately yearned for the satisfaction I got from leading other women to Jesus. I just couldn't come to terms with the loss. That's how my blog ShiftingMyPerspective.com became my focus. Once a week, I'd write a post about some problem I was facing in my motherhood that I knew other moms were struggling with too. Then, I'd find a verse from the Bible that helped me look at the problem in a new light. Inevitably, looking through the lens of Scripture, I'd see the solution God was leading me to.

With each post I put up, more moms commented on how much the blog was helping them. So I kept on writing. One thing led to another, and I began getting writing contracts for different publications and devotionals. With each new contract, things began to make more and more sense. Before, in the retreats, I was helping just a few moms at a time connect with Jesus, all while depleting my own resources. Now, through my writing, I'm able to reach so many more women without expending any physical energy at all. That confirmed for me that writing was my new calling.

• • •

God's true calling never strips us of what we need to carry it out. Instead, it comes with a miracle in math: We end up multiplied, possessing more than what we started with, no matter how much we give away. The exclamation point was put on things when a few random events led to a book contract for *Grace in Tension: Discover Peace with Martha and Mary.* Not only did my first book grow from the content of one of my most sought-after retreats, but it is the fruition of all the lessons God has been teaching me through the years.

Moreover, as I wrote the manuscript, I heard Jesus shift my calling yet again. Rather than use the book to fish for just moms, He asked me to expand my net, casting it farther to fish for everyone and bring them to Him.

Whether male or female, young or old, married or single, with children or without, no one escapes stress on this side of heaven. Jesus yearns to help all of us navigate our tension and transform it into grace at His feet. God never sends us our hardships, but He does show up in the midst of them. When we seek Him out, He always leads us through. God led me through the twists and turns of my medical hardship, helping me realize it was time to find a new path. Now that I'm living out my new calling as a writer, I feel Him bless me with every word I write.

Prayer for a Hope-Filled Life

Mighty Fisher of Men, thank You for the ways You redirect us so our efforts cast the net farther to draw more people to You. Amen.

Whether you turn to the right or to the left, your ears will hear a voice behind you, saying, "This is the way; walk in it."

Isaiah 30:21 (NIV)

TURNED AROUND IN THE DESERT

By Lynne Hartke

"THIS CAN'T BE THE TRAIL," I said to my husband, Kevin, as we hiked in the Superstition Mountains in Arizona. I brushed past another bush, all prickers and thorns. To add insult to injury, even the grass had claws, grabbing my legs when I got too close, leaving behind a mess of red scratches and scrapes.

"I want to keep going a few more minutes," Kevin replied as he bushwhacked through the desert. "The trail should be up in front of us."

A few more minutes turned into ten. Then twenty. Then thirty. My socks collected countless burrs. While Kevin climbed up the rocky embankment of a desert arroyo to check again for a nonexistent trail, I pulled cactus bits from Mollie's fur. Her long terrier-retriever fur was a debris magnet.

I gazed around. The ridgelines dotted with saguaro, prickly pear cactus, and sage all looked the same to me. The temperature had plummeted from a rainstorm the night before, luring us to a final jaunt in the Superstitions before the thermometer would scorch over one hundred degrees in the upcoming summer months. We had been about nine miles into a planned fourteen-mile hike before we got turned around, a hike one friend called one heck-of-a-loop excursion.

• • •

I welcomed the day out in the desert after spending time the week before with a friend and her husband at the hospital.

"The doctor says my husband's cancer has advanced," my friend had said when we stepped out into the hallway. "It's spread to his bones. Is it wrong to still hope?"

After losing both my parents and Kevin's to the disease, I knew the struggle she faced. When medical science runs out of options, do we still cling to a belief in the impossible? Do we still whisper prayers for a miracle? Is it wrong to still hope when doctors have no answers?

I had no answers either.

I had witnessed the long battle our friends had fought with the wretched disease. Surgeries. Chemo. Radiation. Positive scans. Weakened immunity. They had endured an entire roller coaster ride of emotions and longed to just unbuckle the safety belt and step away.

As weeks of treatment turned to months, I found myself struggling to stay connected with my friends. I wanted to step away too—distance myself from their struggle and pain. What could I possibly do for them to bring relief? To provide hope?

Should I bring another meal? Offer to clean their house? Send a funny card? Nothing seemed appropriate any longer and, in my worry to do the wrong thing, I found myself paralyzed from making any decision at all. I was as lost and bewildered as I currently was in the middle of the desert.

"Where is Weavers Needle?" I asked, referring to a thousand-foot spire, a prominent landmark and reference point in this section of the Superstition Wilderness Area. Not only was Weavers Needle a popular photographer destination, but it also lured adventurers seeking the legendary gold buried beneath its shadow. We had enjoyed views of the needle throughout the morning, as we hiked through the desert landscape, passing canyon ragweed, bur sage, and jojoba bushes with their waxy teardrop leaves pointing upward.

"There's the needle," I had said multiple times throughout the day.

"Yep, there it is," Kevin had replied.

We both found comfort in the familiar rock formation, like a beacon of hope, reassuring us we were on the right track. Then we had taken a wrong turn in a desert wash and had lost our point of reference.

• • •

Just breathe, I told myself. *People get in trouble when they panic.* I dug an old comb out of my backpack and combed a segment of jumping cholla cactus out of Mollie's tail. I flung it to the side. *It is not Kevin's fault,* I reminded myself. I swallowed down a biting remark. *Getting upset won't solve anything.*

I tossed Mollie a piece of a bagel from my food pouch. Content with dried kibble at home, Mollie preferred a sandwich on our long hikes, with an occasional hunk of beef jerky thrown in by Kevin for good measure. After a long drink from her collapsible water bowl, we watched Kevin return from his scouting exhibition.

"We need to turn around," Kevin said, skirting around another thorn bush as he descended back into the wash. He pulled out his compass and a topographical map.

"Go back?" I gulped, astonished. My husband never went back. Onward and forward was his life's motto.

"I think we are in the wrong ravine. I couldn't see any trails ahead," he said. He pointed to a squiggle on the topographical map. "We need to go back to where we know where we are."

Understanding nothing about topographical squiggles, but trusting in Kevin's sense of direction, we turned around. At each shallow puddle, Mollie immersed herself in the cool water while we attempted to piece together our backward movements, not wanting to miss the spot where we had made a wrong turn.

"I remember this," Kevin said, pointing to an old saguaro.

"Here's a footprint," I said. Thanks to the rain the night before, ours were the only marks in the soft earth. As

Kevin circled around another cactus, I was convinced our footprints were the only steps ever to come down this off-the-trail arroyo.

"Maybe the recent rain will have washed up that legendary gold by the needle," I said. "We could be rich."

"I'll just be happy when we see the needle again," Kevin said as he lifted a low palo verde branch so I could avoid the thorns. "I am ready to see something I recognize."

We trudged another mile, stopping twice to pull cactus thorns from Mollie's paws. When I had about given up hope, we came to the edge of the wash, to a stack of rocks marking the spot where three trails converged.

"Here's where we took the wrong turn," Kevin said, stepping up to the cairn placed by past hikers to point the way. He pulled out his compass and topographical map to double-check. "Was it really that simple? We went left when we should have stayed to the right."

"And there's Weavers Needle," I said, relieved to see the rock formation in the distance. I was ready to walk on familiar paths.

Do the same with your friend.

What do You mean? I questioned.

Walk on familiar paths.

• • •

The quiet words from Jesus, inside my heart, made me reconsider the distance I had placed between me and my friend and her husband with cancer. I had not wanted to get too close, after having walked the path of illness and grief with all four of our parents.

I had wandered off on side trails to protect myself, but the Spirit of God was pointing me back to the cairn where I had gotten off track. I sensed a gentle invitation to return to what I knew, even though I was afraid.

I didn't have answers, but that was OK. I was not powerless. I could be a carrier of hope, reminding my friends they were not alone.

"Ready to head home?" Kevin asked as he stepped around the cairn to a well-worn path, made smooth by the footsteps of many who had gone before us. Mollie danced ahead, her tail wagging. She wasn't the only one eager to be rid of cactus-strewn adventures.

"Yes," I said, facing the needle, grateful for the familiar landmark to guide our feet home. We had found our way once we had turned around. When I got to the car, I would call my friend and stop in for a visit.

Prayer for a Hope-Filled Life

Dear Jesus, when I hear Your voice, whether to the left or the right, behind me, or in front of me, help me move toward it, as a carrier of hope.

APPLYING GOD'S

No temptation has overtaken you except what is common to mankind. And God is faithful; he will not let you be tempted beyond what you can bear. But when you are tempted, he will also provide a way out so that you can endure it.

1 Corinthians 10:13 (NIV)

THAT LAST SLICE OF CAKE. New shoes. Another glass of wine or pack of cigarettes.

Temptations come in all shapes and sizes, with one to fit every mood or occasion. The mere word itself can induce fantasies of wealth, fame, and power. We're vulnerable. When Eve and Adam shared that piece of fruit, temptation met compromise and—boom—the rest is history.

Like fish in a pond, the bait we're offered seems custom-made to reel us in. Could that explain the placement of chocolate near grocery store registers, or computer algorithms recognizing my need for a new jacket long before I'm aware of it?

The Bible is filled with stories about people like us, from David to Elijah to Joseph—even Jesus. How many of them succeeded in every struggle to win over various enticements? Only One. Like Him, when the others succeeded, it's because they kept their focus on God and the purpose He'd chosen for their lives. When they did fail, they repented, and God forgave.

How can we break free from poor choices? How can we strengthen our resolve to walk away from temptation? There are lessons to be learned from those in the Bible, from our past, and from people we know. We can spend time studying the Bible. We can talk to God, praying to Him for guidance.

And we can forgive ourselves when we make a mistake. After all, God does.

God understands that we aren't perfect, and He offers us a way out through the forgiveness of our sins. Through God, we have the capacity to say "no" to destructive desires and "yes" to hope. And we can trust Him.

—Heidi Gaul

The Lord your God is in your midst, a mighty one who will save; he will rejoice over you with gladness; he will quiet you by his love; he will exult over you with loud singing.

Zephaniah 3:17 (ESV)

MUSIC TO GOD'S EARS

By Linda S. Clare

REVEREND JANE was young, full of faith and energy. She even rode her bike to work. Our new assistant minister had a great sense of humor and felt called to serve God. Plus, she was open about her profound hearing loss. Only a few years before, she'd been fitted with a cochlear implant. She could hear and understand speech well, even if some older folks insisted on raising their voices when speaking to her, as if she were stone deaf.

The day our congregation hired her, I was especially excited. I'm a disabled woman, so I was happy to feel represented on both counts.

Before motherhood, I'd been a church choir member and wedding singer. I even sang semi-professionally for a time. Later, when my four children were young, I worshipped God by singing praise songs as I did housework or while driving the kids to school. Three of my children often rolled their eyes at my efforts, but one son always covered his ears as if in pain, howling at me to stop. He was diagnosed with a hypersensitivity sensory processing disorder. He also battled crippling anxiety. As his sensitivity to sound worsened, I eventually stopped singing, hoping things would change.

• • •

By the time Rev. Jane arrived, I'd given up music except on Sundays. Yet I wanted to make her feel welcomed and understood. One week after services, I offered my own disability story. "I was one of the last children to get polio before the vaccines came along," I told her. "Even though I have permanent arm paralysis, I've raised four kids and manage to do most everything I need to do." I smiled. "Got to appear normal, you know."

Jane strapped on her bike helmet. "I hear you," she said, chuckling. "Get it?"

I laughed. Jane's speech wasn't hard to understand, although her voice did sound somewhat muffled or hollow.

"When did you get your implant?"

"Just a few years ago, actually. The first word I heard was *ketchup*. I was at the dinner table with my family. Someone said, 'Pass the ketchup.'"

"Wow." I tried to seem nonchalant as I focused on the small piece of hardware sitting behind her ear. "Is it like a hearing aid?"

Again, she chortled. "Oh no. Much more complicated than hearing aids. I thank God for the implant every day."

As Jane rode off, I wondered what it was like to hear through a cochlear implant. Did my voice sound like a robot to her? And what would it sound like if she decided to sing?

A few Sundays later, my son and I had a run-in at home. Thinking he wasn't within earshot, I warmed up my singing voice. As I ran through some scales, my son rushed in, howling, "My ears! You're killing my ears!"

I stopped abruptly. "I'm sorry, I didn't think you could hear me." I opened my arms for a hug, but he shrank back.

"I see that you're really upset," I said calmly. "I need to leave for church now, but I'll try not to hurt your ears anymore." He nodded, his hands still covering his ears.

• • •

I walked into the sanctuary with my heart practically dragging on the floor. I sank into my usual spot, still reeling from my son's outburst. But soon I began to feel surrounded by love, love that promised to ease my sorrow. I opened my hymnal, and tearfully sang along with the congregation.

The service cycled through familiar parts. Then Rev. Jane stood up. Instead of speaking the eucharistic prayer as she normally did, our new assistant began to sing.

She threw her whole heart into her effort. But the sound was tuneless—painful even. People exchanged glances that mimicked my son's, although no one dared cover their ears. Every mangled note and off-key sound made me wince. To a music lover like me, the performance was torture. As Rev. Jane continued, people fidgeted in their seats and rustled their bulletins. I found myself begging God to let her finish quickly. And never try to sing again.

Suddenly, I felt God's presence all around me, humbling me, giving me compassion for her. It was as if God Himself was singing. It seemed as if a sacred hush fell over the entire congregation.

Now, instead of praying that something would suddenly stop her singing, I prayed for others to see the beauty God put on display. How many times had I told my son to always try his best? And how many times had I felt embarrassed when my own best wasn't good enough?

By the time Rev. Jane was finished with the prayer, my heart swelled with admiration for her gutsy approach to life. Neither of us had realistic hopes of being "cured" of our disabilities in this life, but I had renewed hope that God would help me through whatever obstacle I faced if only I had the courage to place my hope in Him.

I thought of all the times I'd shied away from doing activities that called attention to my arm's paralysis. I often felt desperate to appear normal. Instead of attempting many "two-handed" skills, such as piano playing, I claimed I wasn't interested. Ashamed of what I viewed as a deformity, I hid my arm's paralysis beneath long sleeves and invented little hacks to cope with a two-handed world.

My heart ached as I thought of my son's disability. Instead of encouraging his strengths, I'd made his sensitivity to sound into a war—my singing versus his ears.

• • •

Jane's foray into singing had taught me important lessons. First, I could be the person God had created without shame. Jane not only admitted her limitations—she embraced them, holding up her hearing loss to God to use in whatever way He chose. Second, she wasn't afraid to try difficult things. I could work on accepting both my own and my son's disabilities, becoming grateful instead of resenting our limitations.

Most importantly, Jane had learned to place her hope and trust in God—not in people's reactions. Instead of constant warring with my son over sound, I could get creative to help us both be content. My hope refreshed itself as I found a sisterhood with this unlikely minister.

The congregation filed out quietly, as if no one knew what to say. Maybe we were more used to being entertained at church than to witnessing God at work. Still, everyone seemed to sense that they'd just been part of something holy. One by one, people stepped up to thank Rev. Jane for her courage. She graciously smiled and shook their hands.

I hung at the back of the receiving line. When I finally stepped up to greet Rev. Jane, tears again flowed. But this time I cried for joy. I thanked her, saying, "Today you proved to me that God always makes a way, if we hope in Him." Walking out to my car, I sang a song of praise and on the way home, I stopped to purchase a pair of noise-canceling headphones for my son. Now I hope for peace between me and my son, a peace like music to God's ears.

Prayer for a Hope-Filled Life

Lord, help me to grow more compassionate toward my limitations and those of others, that I might have the courage to give hope to others.

He heals the brokenhearted and binds up their wounds.

Psalm 147:3 (NIV)

HEALING PROMISES

By Amy Wallace

THE PILLS IN MY HAND SHOOK. Six more inches and I could wipe away fifteen years of pain. I sat in my tiny bedroom and stared out the window at a perfect blue sky with sunlight streaming into the darkness of my life. What a contrast. Beauty outside, just out of my reach. Pain inside, all I could feel.

At fifteen, I wasn't sure what exactly brought me to this moment. It had been a normal week in a normal month, but my life was not normal. I had lived every day in terror of abuse. Since the age of two, I'd been abused in many life-crushing ways. I learned to cope, to be quiet and invisible in order to avoid as much verbal and physical violence as I could. I stayed away from most people because I was never sure who was safe. Staying invisible was relatively easy; I was a military kid who had no real home, and the family I loved had too much pain in their own hearts to see me or love me the way I longed to be loved. I longed for someone who would never raise their voice or their hand to me again. My bar for love was pretty low.

After minutes or an hour of staring at the white pills in my hand, recounting all the memories that brought me to this moment, I grabbed the pill bottle on my dresser. I don't know why I put the pills away. There was no logical reason, nothing to look forward to in the coming week, but I knew ending my life wasn't the answer. I still wasn't sure what was.

The weird weekend passed, and I returned to high school on Monday, to German class, an easy A because I'd grown up in Germany. The class would have been fun, except for this annoying girl who decided we were going to be friends. That should have filled me with hope—a lonely kid longing for someone who wants to be their friend. Unfortunately, this girl only wanted to talk about Jesus.

I listened and was sure her Jesus was too good to be true. Someone who created me and loved me and wanted me to spend my life and eternity with Him? No one wanted me now. I was an abused kid, told I was a disappointment almost daily, reminded by many a boy that I was trash and no one would ever want to be with someone as messed up as me.

Just like the day I had spent with pills in my hand and then put them away, I felt compelled to go to church with Sandra. It made no sense. My parents were against it and wouldn't take me, but Sandra picked me up and took me to church. For weeks, people from church offered me rides every time the doors were open. After a while, though, even they grew tired of all my questions, all my doubts.

I was a disappointment again. This time at church, the one place I'd stupidly hoped I would find a way to belong, to fit in.

• • •

Another Sunday, not too many weeks later, I sat on a stoop outside of the church, again staring into a blue sky and wondering why I kept breathing. Not even this Jesus seemed to want me. People who knew Him well were frustrated every time I asked another question. They didn't understand how scary hope and love were to a kid who'd learned to live without them.

A guy named Chris saw me sitting on the stoop and began a conversation. I started to ask another question, but the words wouldn't come. All I could say was, "I just don't understand any of this Jesus stuff."

Chris's reply was simple: "You won't until you trust Him. He loves you."

He loves me? That couldn't be true. Later, my prayer to God was simple and as shaky as my hands. "I believe You are real, but do You really love me? Me? All broken and unwanted me?"

I heard no answer, but I couldn't stop praying at that point. It was as if I had to say the words that terrified me. Like putting the pills away weeks before, I had to keep praying. "If You really do want me, if You really do love me, if what Your Bible says is true, then I want You. Clean out my heart, forgive me for my sin, save me, Jesus. Please accept me and love me. Will You?"

In that moment, I was flooded with a love so pure, so perfect, so unimaginable, something I had never, ever experienced before. "Jesus Loves Me" wasn't just a song. It was true. Jesus loved me. Me. The broken, unwanted, invisible girl was now seen and wanted and there was hope of healing. No one but Jesus could heal my broken pieces. He promised He would.

The shattered pieces of my life didn't instantly mend. I was still an abused kid in a dangerous world, but little by little I stopped being invisible. I made a few friends at church and at school. I dove into the Bible and Bible studies; I sang in the choir and traveled with the church group all across the United States and into Canada. I started to trust a few people.

I trusted a few wrong people too. I dated a guy who my friends didn't like, but I didn't listen. He went to church. He didn't look or act like my primary abusers, so I thought I'd be OK. I wasn't. I ignored the nudging of the Lord to get out of the relationship, and I was hurt again in a way no human should be hurt. Once again, I heard the words that I was trash...unwanted...worthless.

This time, I ran to Jesus with no questions, only hurt without words. "Do You still love me? Will You reject me too?" Like my first prayer, Jesus answered with overwhelming, unimaginable, perfect love and spoke to my heart these word from His Word: "You are My beloved child."

Jesus loved me. In that moment, that was enough to keep putting one foot in front of the other.

• • •

I wish I could say there were no more poor choices and healing was a journey ever upward and filled with joy. It wasn't. Every victory was hard fought; every loss, painful; every failure, crushing; and every hurt threatened my hope of healing. But I held onto what I knew to be true: Jesus loved me.

I graduated at the top of my class in high school and college. I got married and raised three amazing children. All the while, what kept me going was the reminder that I was and am God's beloved child. He sees me. He loves me. He is healing me. He has promised to complete the work He began. And I know and trust He keeps His promises.

Prayer for a Hope-Filled Life

Jesus, You are Healer and Hope. You love and receive and heal Your children. Thank You! Help us trust You and receive the hope and healing promised in You. Amen.

To them God chose to make known how great among the Gentiles are the riches of the glory of this mystery, which is Christ in you, the hope of glory.

Colossians 1:27 (ESV)

HOPE IN THE MIDST OF CHAOS

By Heather Jepsen

WE ALL HAVE HAD DAYS that do not go according to plan. Sometimes it feels like anything that can go wrong will go wrong. When one small thing is thrown off course, with faith and practice, we can dust ourselves off and keep going. But when everything happens at once and everything goes wrong, it can be hard to find hope.

Like many mothers, I have had some bad days. But one recent day was among the worst. It started off rough with grumpy kids. It was all I could do to get everyone out the door and in the car on time for school. Just a few minutes into the drive, the kids started arguing in the back. I lost my cool. "Knock it off, you two!" I yelled, only to instantly regret it. Whenever things seem to go wrong with the kids, I always feel like such a failure.

Finally, the kids were dropped off and settled in and I returned home for a cup of coffee. I know I can spin out of control when I get stressed, so I try to plan some quiet prayer moments in each day. When the to-do list is long, prayer can take a bottom rung. But when I make prayer a priority, then at least I start each day with God, beginning every day on the right foot if I can.

That morning I was reading in the book of Romans. Paul was writing about community and how we need to welcome each other in the name of God. Had I welcomed my children that morning? Or my husband, who was still in bed since he was working the night shift that week? Was I doing good work for building up my community, or only being a crabby morning mom? My prayer that morning was that God would be with me: "Lord, help me find peace in this day. Help me to know You are with me."

• • •

Off I went to work, hoping for a better day, only to wander into the storm that is my job. I am a small-town pastor, and this day, like many others, had me spread thin. My stress level was high. There were tensions at church over the budget, and as usual, we had less money than we wished we had. Was I going to go out and ask for more donations? Or could I find a place to cut back on our expenses? These business matters were not part of my spiritual training. I prayed, "Lord, how am I supposed to do this?" I kept coming back to Paul's letter to the Romans. Community is the key, Paul seemed to say. Community is the way to hope.

As the day went on, I got more frazzled. Too much to do and too little time to do it all. I stressed about trying to do everything right. At the same time, I kept coming back to that idea from Romans. "Isn't the steadfast love of God enough? Why can't I just let go and let God?"

My last order of work for the day was a visit with some members of my church. They lived in the country, way out of town, and so it would be at least thirty minutes each way to drive out and back. This church couple were so sweet, and they were some of my favorite people. I usually enjoy our visits, but I could tell right off that something was wrong. They looked so tired, and the home was not as clean as it usually was. It seemed the husband, Charles, was beginning to forget things, and his wife Bertha's health was on the decline.

I tried to broach the subject of in-home help or possibly moving into a facility, but they wouldn't hear of it. "Lord, help me," I prayed. Could I encourage these folks to make different choices? I didn't want to hurt feelings, but I also didn't want to ignore problems I was noticing. It was heartbreaking, and I felt helpless. Sometimes it can be hard to find hope when all I see every day is the despair of life.

As I drove home, I felt sad and frustrated. What a horrible day this had turned out to be. Suddenly the phone rang. It was my husband, and he was frantic on the line: "I dropped a glass bowl in the sink, and it shattered. I cut my hand."

I asked him how bad it was.

"Pretty bad. I can't stop the bleeding."

Ugh, I thought, *what am I going to do?*

My husband could not drive with a heavily bleeding hand, and I was too far away to make it in time to get him to the hospital and pick the kids up from school. Suddenly I had an idea—community! Paul had been talking about community, and I had a church community I could call. I phoned one of my best deacons, Sharon, and pleaded with her, "I know this is a strange request, but would you please go to my house, get Lars, and give him a ride to the ER?" Miraculously she agreed.

I zipped back to town and went straight to the ER. There I met my husband and surveyed the damage. It was bad—five stitches in his finger—but he was going to be OK. While I sat keeping him company, the phone rang. It was my son's school and my heart dropped. "Oh Lord, now what?"

I stepped outside and answered the phone. It was Henry's first-grade teacher, calling to report that he was in the principal's office. It seems he had gotten mad at another child during group work in class and had proceeded to twist her arm in his frustration. It is very embarrassing when the pastor's kid gets in trouble at school. Luckily, she said, she was confident that Henry understood the error of his ways. He would be released at the end of the school day to apologize to the girl and then I could pick him up. "Just let me finish up in the ER," I said, "and I will be right there." *Lord, have mercy,* I prayed under my breath.

I left Lars to finish his stitches and ran off to the school to get my son and daughter. Coming home, I knew I would be facing a mess. If my husband had cut himself at the kitchen sink, then blood would be everywhere. But to my wonder, when I came home, the kitchen had been cleaned. "How did this happen?" I asked.

"Must have been Sharon," my husband replied.

After I got everyone settled in, including my son in his room for a time out, I phoned Sharon.

"Yes," she said, "it was me. I picked Lars up and saw what a mess it was. I knew you were stressed when you called, and still had the kids to get, so I came back here after I dropped him off and cleaned things up."

"Sharon, you are a saint," I said. "You don't know how much this means to me."

"I know," she said. "You care for us, and we care for you. That's what being a church community is all about."

As I hung up the phone, I thought back to the start of my day and the reading from Paul. Paul finds hope in community, and it was the communities of church and family that brought me comfort throughout the day. With the help of my community, even the worst day turned into an opportunity to find hope in the midst of chaos.

Prayer for a Hope-Filled Life

Dear God, when things go wrong, help me to find hope in You. Even in the midst of chaos, may I be grounded in faith and hope. Amen.

In their hearts humans plan their course, but the LORD establishes their steps.

Proverbs 16:9 (NIV)

PLANS. FOR MANY OF US, that word can be a double-edged sword. We wrap our hopes and dreams in the tissue-thin belief that we can make them come true, all on our own. Soon, those plans we've made can become a dreadful source of anxiety and regret. We look back on the past and shake our heads over messy mistakes we've made. Then we turn to the future and set out once again to make things happen according to our wishes.

Although the Lord's Prayer was written thousands of years ago to teach people to pray, its words are appropriate to all of us today. In this case, it reminds us that God is in charge, that He makes the plans for our life, not us. In the lines "Thy kingdom come, Thy will be done," we are asking that God's ways happen here, in our lives, as they are in heaven. And then that God's will occurs—that we align our will to God's will and submit ourselves to Him.

Those words include a future full of hope that He has made plans for our future. Isn't that astonishing? These plans don't focus on beauty, youth, strength, power, or riches. Nor do they reflect any of the world's definitions of accomplishment or success. Instead, they are built on God's promise of prosperity—His plans to give us hope and a future.

Try to imagine perfect, endless prosperity. Beyond posing as an overwhelming concept, it paints a reality we'd do well to accept—plans to prosper you and not to harm you. Just the thought brings a smile to my face and a sense of security in my heart.

—Heidi Gaul

The LORD said to him, "Who gave human beings their mouths? Who makes them deaf or mute? Who gives them sight or makes them blind? Is it not I, the LORD? Now go; I will help you speak and will teach you what to say."

Exodus 4:11–12 (NIV)

FROM TONGUE-TIED TO TENACIOUS

By Bettie Boswell

GULPING FOR AIR, I looked out on a class of college freshmen and began fumbling my way through a speech about piano history. Focusing on the papers in front of me prevented any discouraging effects from a yawning audience. I'd prayed for courage, but at the moment all I could think about was how soon the torture would end. Graduation for this senior couldn't come soon enough.

I'd delayed taking Public Speaking 101 as long as I could. Since the class was a Bible college requirement, the time to face the teeming masses had finally arrived. In other courses, I'd never raised my hand to answer questions. It was easier to whisper the answer and let another student have the attention. This class didn't provide me a similar escape. My hopes centered on survival as the semester passed in a blur of nerves and nightmares about speaking in front of others. Somehow, I survived and managed to pass the subject, ready for a diploma in church music after my last music-related challenge.

• • •

As a music student I enjoyed singing God's glories in the choir, surrounded by supportive voices. Standing solo on any stage was a different matter, whether in the dreaded speech class or for my senior recital. I somehow managed to forget about advertising that final musical event, hoping no one would discover my omission. The only attendees were my fiancé, his roommate, my mother, and a couple of professors. Great relief filled me when I saw the small crowd. I was still thankful for the formal dress hiding my wobbling legs. However, nerves do help the voice have a nice shaking tremolo. God had given me the gift of a tone-filled voice that night. He used my fright to glorify Him in song. Maybe there was hope for me beyond the hallowed halls of academia.

Graduation came and went. I got married and found a satisfying part-time job behind the scenes at a store. Not having to deal directly with customers or be outgoing was an answer to prayer. I could work by organizing goods or doing simple bookkeeping—no speeches required. Singing in the church choir still satisfied my need to serve the Lord. But God and my preacher husband had other plans.

One quiet Saturday afternoon, my husband held out a slip of paper with a phone number on it. "Hey, honey, I need you to do me a favor. Please call this woman and invite her to come back to church." I stepped back like he'd offered me a wriggling viper. Did he even realize how much fear had reared up in my chest at that moment?

"I'm not very good at talking to people. I'll clean the church, or help type the bulletin, or..." He pressed the phone number into my palm. There didn't seem to be a choice. I prayed for help. It turned out the delinquent church member gladly received the call. After my stuttering introduction and invitation to church, she started chatting. From that point on, an occasional "yes" or "OK" from me was sufficient for an hour-long "conversation." God had answered my prayer in a special way, giving me a new friend who more than made up for my quiet personality. But He wasn't finished. I'd only taken a first step.

• • •

The next path in my journey, to untie my tongue and timidity, took place at work. At that time, I was a happy introvert who counted inventory and reported numbers weekly to the boss. Then a most dreaded change in modern technology ravaged my job. Who knew that a computer would rob me of my solitary position? The business graciously moved me to a retail buyer's front desk as a secretary. My heart sank. But God and the company pushed me forward on my journey as I started answering calls from New York clients and dissatisfied customers. Daily practice grew my confidence. I was making progress and began to realize I could do this, when required. When my children were born, leaving work to care for them was a nice retreat from the busy world.

Stepping back didn't last long, though. When no Sunday school class existed for my youngsters, I took on the challenge. My God-given maternal drive gave me courage to create and teach lessons. Sharing Jesus with the little ones filled me with purpose. During the years of staying at home, my joy of serving the children stretched into leading vacation Bible schools and youth activities. I forgot about being self-conscious while teaching children. Unbeknownst to me, these opportunities were providing a hope for my future.

Those years of staying at home had taken a toll on our budget. The need to return to a paying position was imminent once our children were of preschool age. I thought the only opportunity would be in another retail position. This time it was my husband who suggested other plans. He saw my growing talent for working with children.

"You should get a teaching degree."

After a moment of panic, I realized he was right. Once again, I took a position in the background, but that work would provide a stepping stone into a new vocation. My new job was at a university, where I would work my way through a master's degree in education.

• • •

I began to see that I didn't have to worry about speaking in front of adults anymore. Most of my fellow students were much younger, mere children in my eyes. Many of the professors were too. Those adults were looking more and more like the little ones I loved teaching at church. God gave me the power to overcome my weakness. It flowed through my veins and sometimes out of my mouth.

Making the professors answer questions, whether or not they wanted to do so, became a priority. I wanted to make the most of my education. My younger classmates thanked me on several occasions for making instructors clarify confusing topics. During a math class, the professor informed us that our ending grades would represent a true bell curve with only a few students receiving A's. That semester we proved him wrong because he had to explain each concept in detail due to questions asked. Quite a few students attained the A grade. My philosophy became: "Ask questions." I realized if I am persistent, I will receive an answer. I was changing from fearful to focused, from doubtful to hopeful.

I added a license in music to my elementary education teaching degree after I took the required class on music for classroom teachers. The instructor happened to be a former professor at the Bible college I attended. He shared the good news that I only needed to take three classes to add a music certification. When I completed his music class, he asked me to be his substitute instructor. I didn't hesitate. I stepped right up and taught his classes with the same joy I had when teaching my little ones at church.

Not only did the opportunity provide a little extra income, but the experiences made me realize how far I had come. My knees no longer knocked together in fear. Hiding behind something or someone was part of the past. When graduation came, I left with hope for the future. My love of music remained from before, but now it held confidence. I also had a new voice, that of a classroom teacher. God provided two options for my teaching career. He knew I would need both when changes came in my husband's ministry.

During thirty-three years of teaching, I taught in both general music and elementary classrooms. I also instructed courses for colleges on a part-time basis. Teaching students in private and public schools, I gave my all, in a way that witnessed the Lord in my life to those students. The shy quiet students had special places in my heart, since I understood them well.

My hope had changed from wanting to avoid difficult situations to knowing that with God, all things hoped for are possible. Thanks to God's care and a few pushes from my husband, I went from a tongue-tied student to a teacher with plenty to say.

Prayer for a Hope-Filled Life

Dear Heavenly Father, help me to accept and recognize the hope You offer when I am trying to overcome a weakness. In Jesus's Name, Amen.

Have I not commanded you? Be strong and courageous. Do not be afraid; do not be discouraged, for the LORD your God will be with you wherever you go.

Joshua 1:9 (NIV)

STRONG AND COURAGEOUS

By Chris Maday Schmidt

R. C. SPROUL ONCE SAID, "Hope is called the anchor of the soul because it gives stability to the Christian life.... It is that which latches on to the certainty of the promises of the future that God has made."

Little did I know how true this would prove in my own life eighteen years and some odd days ago on an ordinary August evening in Arizona with triple-digit temperatures. My twelve-year-old daughter, Bailey, and I had been waiting for my husband, Bob, to get home from work at seven o'clock for a family bike ride. Except that seven o'clock came and went with no sign of him.

Assuming Bob was simply running late or stuck in heavy rush-hour traffic, I left a quick message on his mobile voice mail.

"You're not here, so Bailey and I are running to the library." Our preteen and I piled into the car and made the round trip in forty-five minutes. But upon our return home, the sun sinking closer toward the horizon, the garage stalls remained empty.

"Mom."

Within that one word couched in a tone of uncertainty, I sensed a wealth of unasked questions and concerns. And because it wasn't like Bob to be that late—especially without a heads-up—I couldn't stop the niggle of dread that had begun to inch up my spine.

"I know."

Yet as a believer for more than a decade of my life, I also knew that worrying wasn't the answer.

Once inside our home, I tried Bob's cell phone again and ended up in voice mail. "It's almost eight. Are you on your way?" I also tried his office number with the same result.

"He must've gotten tied up at work," I asserted aloud, choosing to speak life and believe the best.

• • •

The Olympics were in full swing that year, so I suggested Bailey tune into the games as we waited for her dad. While she settled herself on the family room sofa in front of the TV,

I called my girlfriend Tammy and mentioned Bob's tardiness. Several minutes into our conversation, the doorbell rang.

Admittedly, at the sound, the strong sense that something was wrong swept through me again. While Tammy waited on the other end of the line, I peered through the peephole into the muted glow illuminating our front porch. I could just make out a man in uniform and two women.

My pulse thundered in my ears as I cracked open the door and blurted the first thing that popped into my mind. "I don't think I want to talk to you."

Searching the officer's eyes for answers, I became faintly aware that Bailey was no longer in the family room, but instead was standing on the staircase behind me.

"It's not as bad as you think," the officer said.

How did he know what I was thinking? With trembling fingers, I unlocked the storm door and swung it open, a silent invitation to my three callers. Once inside, the officer quickly pieced together the evening's events. Bailey and I learned that two hours earlier, an intoxicated driver behind the wheel of a full-size pickup had T-boned Bob's four-door sedan. Following life-saving measures at the scene of the crash, he'd then been air-lifted to a level I trauma center thirty miles away.

Fast-forward to the hospital several hours later, after Bob had undergone emergency surgery. No television show nor Hollywood film could have prepared me for the sight of my unconscious and battered husband lying in an ICU bed—his body hooked up to noisy machines that drained fluid from his lungs and monitored his vitals.

Nor could I have imagined the bleak litany of injuries his attending nurse would rattle off, including traumatic brain injury, crushed hip, broken ribs, a punctured lung, and a displaced clavicle.

Yet despite the dark valley that stretched in front of me, something shifted in my spirit that night when a small voice whispered a command to be strong and courageous—regardless of the circumstances—because the Lord would be with me every step of the way.

It was this promise I clung to each morning I woke in a fetal position, before rolling from my bed to the floor and crying out to God for His help to face another day of unknowns.

And it was this promise that armed me with strength every time I was asked to sign off on another test or procedure, and when Bob's care team ordered a medically induced coma to allow his brain a better chance to heal, as well as when I noticed tremors coursing through Bob's body and called for his attending neurologist.

"It's normal," I was informed.

But when I left the hospital to pick up Bailey at my cousin's home, I relayed the news of Bob's tremors to a group of church parishioners meeting there, after which they prayed over a cloth napkin. The next morning, while Bob slept, I slowly eased the cloth over his body from head to toe. Miraculously, the tremors that had been visible upon my arrival had disappeared.

On one particular morning, while traversing the ICU corridor, I met Bob's head surgeon outside of my husband's room. The doctor greeted me with kind eyes and a friendly smile. "So, about Robert's TBI.... We won't know the extent of his brain trauma for about a year...how goofy he'll end up."

"If you can get him back to his original goofy self," I responded, "I'll take him."

Dr. Wachtel grinned at me, stating that it's possible to get an idea of how strong a person is by the way they handle adversity.

"By the grace of God," I said. It was the only explanation.

• • •

Throughout the fifty-nine days Bob was hospitalized, as well as the subsequent months of outpatient physical therapy, my family learned a lot about God's grace and His promise to never leave us. By sending others to walk alongside us through our dark valley—from the provision of homemade meals and gift cards to school lunches and after-school care for Bailey to extra gas money—we were never alone. There were also the prayer warriors who interceded behind the scenes on our behalf, as well as Bob's colleagues who stopped by to visit, including one sweet woman he worked with who delivered a blanket for me to use during my daily vigils at the hospital.

Then there were the landmark moments we celebrated, each one a stepping stone of hope grounded in our faithful God: Bob's courage as he learned how to walk and talk again, and how to write and feed himself. And when he was released to drive and eventually return to work—something I was told early on by professionals not to expect, but a bridge I vowed to cross if God brought us to it.

Yet even when the days turned to night, oftentimes accompanied by the cries of my heart as I poured out my fears and anxieties, the Holy Spirit reminded me through His Word—fragments of scriptures that ministered to my weary soul—that weeping may last for a night, but joy would come in the morning.

Nearly two decades later, this remains true today. And whenever life's difficulties threaten to discourage me, I remember the Lord's command to me to be strong and courageous all those years ago, followed by His promise. Because if His Word declares that God is the King of heaven's armies, then the battle—and the victory—are His. Evidence that the One who is faithful will do it.

Prayer for a Hope-Filled Life

Lord, help me to recall Your past faithfulness so that when I face circumstances that seem scary or insurmountable, my hope will stand firm on Your promises.

BIBLICAL PROMISES OF HOPE

All scriptures from NIV translation.

Acts 2:38	Peter replied, "Repent and be baptized, every one of you, in the name of Jesus Christ for the forgiveness of your sins. And you will receive the gift of the Holy Spirit.
Acts 24:15	And I have the same hope in God as these men themselves have, that there will be a resurrection of both the righteous and the wicked.
Colossians 1:5	The faith and love that spring from the hope stored up for you in heaven and about which you have already heard in the true message of the gospel.
Colossians 1:23	If you continue in your faith, established and firm, and do not move from the hope held out in the gospel. This is the gospel that you heard and that has been proclaimed to every creature under heaven, and of which I, Paul, have become a servant.
Colossians 1:27	To them God has chosen to make known among the Gentiles the glorious riches of this mystery, which is Christ in you, the hope of glory.
Colossians 3:1–2	Since, then, you have been raised with Christ, set your hearts on things above, where Christ is, seated at the right hand of God. Set your minds on things above, not on earthly things.
1 Corinthians 2:9	However, as it is written: "What no eye has seen, what no ear has heard, and what no human mind has conceived"—the things God has prepared for those who love him.
1 Corinthians 13:6–7	Love does not delight in evil but rejoices with the truth. It always protects, always trusts, always hopes, always perseveres.
1 Corinthians 13:13	And now these three remain: faith, hope and love. But the greatest of these is love.

1 Corinthians 15:19	If only for this life we have hope in Christ, we are of all people most to be pitied.
1 Corinthians 15:21–22	For since death came through a man, the resurrection of the dead comes also through a man. For as in Adam all die, so in Christ all will be made alive.
2 Corinthians 1:10	He has delivered us from such a deadly peril, and he will deliver us again. On him we have set our hope that he will continue to deliver us.
2 Corinthians 1:20	For no matter how many promises God has made, they are "Yes" in Christ. And so through him the "Amen" is spoken by us to the glory of God.
2 Corinthians 3:12	Therefore, since we have such a hope, we are very bold.
2 Corinthians 4:16	Therefore we do not lose heart. Though outwardly we are wasting away, yet inwardly we are being renewed day by day.
2 Corinthians 4:18	So we fix our eyes not on what is seen, but on what is unseen, since what is seen is temporary, but what is unseen is eternal.
2 Corinthians 5:7	For we live by faith, not by sight.
2 Corinthians 5:17	Therefore, if anyone is in Christ, the new creation has come: The old has gone, the new is here!
Deuteronomy 31:6	Be strong and courageous. Do not be afraid or terrified because of them, for the LORD your God goes with you; he will never leave you nor forsake you.
Ephesians 1:18	I pray that the eyes of your heart may be enlightened in order that you may know the hope to which he has called you, the riches of his glorious inheritance in his holy people.
Ephesians 2:8	For it is by grace you have been saved, through faith—and this is not from yourselves, it is the gift of God.

Ephesians 2:12	Remember that at that time you were separate from Christ, excluded from citizenship in Israel and foreigners to the covenants of the promise, without hope and without God in the world.
Ephesians 4:4	There is one body and one Spirit, just as you were called to one hope when you were called.
Galatians 5:5	For through the Spirit we eagerly await by faith the righteousness for which we hope.
Galatians 5:22–23	But the fruit of the Spirit is love, joy, peace, forbearance, kindness, goodness, faithfulness, gentleness and self-control. Against such things there is no law.
Galatians 6:8	Whoever sows to please their flesh, from the flesh will reap destruction; whoever sows to please the Spirit, from the Spirit will reap eternal life.
Hebrews 3:6	But Christ is faithful as the Son over God's house. And we are his house, if indeed we hold firmly to our confidence and the hope in which we glory.
Hebrews 6:11	We want each of you to show this same diligence to the very end, so that what you hope for may be fully realized.
Hebrews 6:19	We have this hope as an anchor for the soul, firm and secure. It enters the inner sanctuary behind the curtain.
Hebrews 10:23	Let us hold unswervingly to the hope we profess, for he who promised is faithful.
Hebrews 11:1	Now faith is confidence in what we hope for and assurance about what we do not see.
Isaiah 40:31	But those who hope in the Lord will renew their strength. They will soar on wings like eagles; they will run and not grow weary, they will walk and not be faint.

Isaiah 41:10	So do not fear, for I am with you; do not be dismayed, for I am your God. I will strengthen you and help you; I will uphold you with my righteous right hand.
Isaiah 65:24	Before they call I will answer; while they are still speaking I will hear.
James 1:12	Blessed is the one who perseveres under trial because, having stood the test, that person will receive the crown of life that the Lord has promised to those who love him.
Jeremiah 17:7	But blessed is the one who trusts in the LORD, whose confidence is in him.
Jeremiah 29:11	"For I know the plans I have for you," declares the LORD, "plans to prosper you and not to harm you, plans to give you hope and a future."
Job 11:18	You will be secure, because there is hope; you will look about you and take your rest in safety.
Job 13:15	Though he slay me, yet will I hope in him; I will surely defend my ways to his face.
Joel 3:16	The LORD will roar from Zion and thunder from Jerusalem; the earth and the heavens will tremble. But the LORD will be a refuge for his people, a stronghold for the people of Israel.
John 3:16	For God so loved the world that he gave his one and only Son, that whoever believes in him shall not perish but have eternal life.
John 11:25–26	Jesus said to her, "I am the resurrection and the life. The one who believes in me will live, even though they die; and whoever lives by believing in me will never die. Do you believe this?"
John 14:27	Peace I leave with you; my peace I give you. I do not give to you as the world gives. Do not let your hearts be troubled and do not be afraid.

1 John 3:3	All who have this hope in him purify themselves, just as he is pure.
1 John 4:18	There is no fear in love. But perfect love drives out fear, because fear has to do with punishment. The one who fears is not made perfect in love.
Lamentations 3:21	Yet this I call to mind and therefore I have hope.
Lamentations 3:24	I say to myself, "The LORD is my portion; therefore I will wait for him."
Luke 1:37	For no word from God will ever fail.
Mark 9:23	"'If you can'?" said Jesus. "Everything is possible for one who believes."
Matthew 7:7–8	Ask and it will be given to you; seek and you will find; knock and the door will be opened to you. For everyone who asks receives; the one who seeks finds; and to the one who knocks, the door will be opened.
Matthew 11:28	Come to me, all you who are weary and burdened, and I will give you rest.
Matthew 12:21	In his name the nations will put their hope.
Matthew 25:21	His master replied, "Well done, good and faithful servant! You have been faithful with a few things; I will put you in charge of many things. Come and share your master's happiness!"
Micah 7:7	But as for me, I watch in hope for the LORD, I wait for God my Savior; my God will hear me.
Numbers 23:19	God is not human, that he should lie, not a human being, that he should change his mind. Does he speak and then not act? Does he promise and not fulfill?
1 Peter 1:3	Praise be to the God and Father of our Lord Jesus Christ! In his great mercy he has given us new birth into a living hope through the resurrection of Jesus Christ from the dead.

1 Peter 1:13	Therefore, with minds that are alert and fully sober, set your hope on the grace to be brought to you when Jesus Christ is revealed at his coming.
1 Peter 1:21	Through him you believe in God, who raised him from the dead and glorified him, and so your faith and hope are in God.
1 Peter 3:15	But in your hearts revere Christ as Lord. Always be prepared to give an answer to everyone who asks you to give the reason for the hope that you have. But do this with gentleness and respect.
1 Peter 4:8	Above all, love each other deeply, because love covers over a multitude of sins.
1 Peter 5:10	And the God of all grace, who called you to his eternal glory in Christ, after you have suffered a little while, will himself restore you and make you strong, firm and steadfast.
Philippians 1:6	Being confident of this, that he who began a good work in you will carry it on to completion until the day of Christ Jesus.
Philippians 3:13–14	Brothers and sisters, I do not consider myself yet to have taken hold of it. But one thing I do: Forgetting what is behind and straining toward what is ahead, I press on toward the goal to win the prize for which God has called me heavenward in Christ Jesus.
Proverbs 10:28	The prospect of the righteous is joy, but the hopes of the wicked come to nothing.
Proverbs 13:12	Hope deferred makes the heart sick, but a longing fulfilled is a tree of life.
Proverbs 23:18	There is surely a future hope for you, and your hope will not be cut off.

Proverbs 24:14	Know also that wisdom is like honey for you: If you find it, there is a future hope for you, and your hope will not be cut off.
Psalm 9:18	But God will never forget the needy; the hope of the afflicted will never perish.
Psalm 10:17	You, LORD, hear the desire of the afflicted; you encourage them, and you listen to their cry.
Psalm 23:1–4	The LORD is my shepherd, I lack nothing. He makes me lie down in green pastures, he leads me beside quiet waters, he refreshes my soul. He guides me along the right paths for his name's sake. Even though I walk through the darkest valley, I will fear no evil, for you are with me; your rod and your staff, they comfort me.
Psalm 25:5	Guide me in your truth and teach me, for you are God my Savior, and my hope is in you all day long.
Psalm 31:24	Be strong and take heart, all you who hope in the LORD.
Psalm 33:18	But the eyes of the LORD are on those who fear him, on those whose hope is in his unfailing love.
Psalm 33:22	May your unfailing love be with us, LORD, even as we put our hope in you.
Psalm 38:15	LORD, I wait for you; you will answer, Lord my God.
Psalm 39:7	But now, Lord, what do I look for? My hope is in you.
Psalm 42:11	Why, my soul, are you downcast? Why so disturbed within me? Put your hope in God, for I will yet praise him, my Savior and my God.
Psalm 46:1-2	God is our refuge and strength, an ever-present help in trouble. Therefore we will not fear, though the earth give way and the mountains fall into the heart of the sea.

Psalm 62:5	Yes, my soul, find rest in God; my hope comes from him.
Psalm 71:5	For you have been my hope, Sovereign Lord, my confidence since my youth.
Psalm 71:14	As for me, I will always have hope; I will praise you more and more.
Psalm 78:7	Then they would put their trust in God and would not forget his deeds but would keep his commands.
Psalm 119:81	My soul faints with longing for your salvation, but I have put my hope in your word.
Psalm 119:114	You are my refuge and my shield; I have put my hope in your word.
Psalm 130:5	I wait for the Lord, my whole being waits, and in his word I put my hope.
Psalm 130:7	Israel, put your hope in the Lord, for with the Lord is unfailing love and with him is full redemption.
Psalm 146:5	Blessed are those whose help is the God of Jacob, whose hope is in the Lord their God.
Psalm 147:11	The Lord delights in those who fear him, who put their hope in his unfailing love.
Revelation 21:4	He will wipe every tear from their eyes. There will be no more death or mourning or crying or pain, for the old order of things has passed away.
Romans 1:16	For I am not ashamed of the gospel, because it is the power of God that brings salvation to everyone who believes: first to the Jew, then to the Gentile.
Romans 4:18	Against all hope, Abraham in hope believed and so became the father of many nations, just as it had been said to him, "So shall your offspring be."

Romans 5:2–5	Through whom we have gained access by faith into this grace in which we now stand. And we boast in the hope of the glory of God. Not only so, but we also glory in our sufferings, because we know that suffering produces perseverance; perseverance, character; and character, hope. And hope does not put us to shame, because God's love has been poured out into our hearts through the Holy Spirit, who has been given to us.
Romans 8:18	I consider that our present sufferings are not worth comparing with the glory that will be revealed in us.
Romans 8:24–25	For in this hope we were saved. But hope that is seen is no hope at all. Who hopes for what they already have? But if we hope for what we do not yet have, we wait for it patiently.
Romans 8:28	And we know that in all things God works for the good of those who love him, who have been called according to his purpose.
Romans 8:31	What, then, shall we say in response to these things? If God is for us, who can be against us?
Romans 8:33	Who will bring any charge against those whom God has chosen? It is God who justifies.
Romans 10:15	And how can anyone preach unless they are sent? As it is written: "How beautiful are the feet of those who bring good news!"
Romans 12:12	Be joyful in hope, patient in affliction, faithful in prayer.
Romans 14:17	For the kingdom of God is not a matter of eating and drinking, but of righteousness, peace and joy in the Holy Spirit.
Romans 15:4	For everything that was written in the past was written to teach us, so that through the endurance taught in the Scriptures and the encouragement they provide we might have hope.

Romans 15:13	May the God of hope fill you with all joy and peace as you trust in him, so that you may overflow with hope by the power of the Holy Spirit.
1 Thessalonians 1:3	We remember before our God and Father your work produced by faith, your labor prompted by love, and your endurance inspired by hope in our Lord Jesus Christ.
1 Thessalonians 4:13	Brothers and sisters, we do not want you to be uninformed about those who sleep in death, so that you do not grieve like the rest of mankind, who have no hope.
1 Thessalonians 5:8	But since we belong to the day, let us be sober, putting on faith and love as a breastplate, and the hope of salvation as a helmet.
1 Timothy 1:1	Paul, an apostle of Christ Jesus by the command of God our Savior and of Christ Jesus our hope.
1 Timothy 4:10	That is why we labor and strive, because we have put our hope in the living God, who is the Savior of all people, and especially of those who believe.
1 Timothy 6:17	Command those who are rich in this present world not to be arrogant nor to put their hope in wealth, which is so uncertain, but to put their hope in God, who richly provides us with everything for our enjoyment.
2 Timothy 1:7	For the Spirit God gave us does not make us timid, but gives us power, love and self-discipline.
Titus 1:2	In the hope of eternal life, which God, who does not lie, promised before the beginning of time.
Titus 2:12–13	It teaches us to say "No" to ungodliness and worldly passions, and to live self-controlled, upright and godly lives in this present age, while we wait for the blessed hope—the appearing of the glory of our great God and Savior, Jesus Christ.

Titus 3:5–7	He saved us, not because of righteous things we had done, but because of his mercy. He saved us through the washing of rebirth and renewal by the Holy Spirit, whom he poured out on us generously through Jesus Christ our Savior, so that, having been justified by his grace, we might become heirs having the hope of eternal life.
Zechariah 9:12	Return to your fortress, you prisoners of hope; even now I announce that I will restore twice as much to you.
Zephaniah 3:17	The LORD your God is with you, the Mighty Warrior who saves. He will take great delight in you; in his love he will no longer rebuke you, but will rejoice over you with singing.

A NOTE FROM THE EDITORS

We hope you enjoyed *Exploring God's Promises: Hope,* published by Guideposts. For over seventy-five years, Guideposts, a nonprofit organization, has been driven by a vision of a world filled with hope. We aspire to be the voice of a trusted friend, a friend who makes you feel more hopeful and connected.

By making a purchase from Guideposts, you join our community in touching millions of lives, inspiring them to believe that all things are possible through faith, hope, and prayer. Your continued support allows us to provide uplifting resources to those in need. Whether through our communities, websites, apps, or publications, we inspire our audiences, bring them together, and comfort, uplift, entertain, and guide them. Visit us at guideposts.org to learn more.

We would love to hear from you. Write us at Guideposts, P.O. Box 5815, Harlan, Iowa 51593 or call us at (800) 932-2145. Did you love *Exploring God's Promises: Hope*? Leave a review for this product on guideposts.org/shop. Your feedback helps others in our community find relevant products.

Printed in the United States
by Baker & Taylor Publisher Services